THE LUGGER COAST

A Review of Working Sail in the West

Vol. 3 The Coast in the Past Series
ROBERT SIMPER.

Published by Creekside Publishing

ISBN 0 9538506 4 1
Copyright Robert Simper 2003
Printed by Lavenham Press Ltd
Lavenham, Suffolk

Robert Simper is one of Britain's best-known writers on traditional working boats. His most acclaimed books have been *Britain's Maritime Heritage*, which became the prototype for many similar books, and *In Search of Sail* which covers his own sailing experience in many parts of the world. He has written the 'Sail Review'column in 'Sea Breezes' for thirty-seven years and has written for 'Classic Boat' since that magazine started at Penryn in 1986. Robert is a member of the Society for Nautical Research and has been much concerned with the boat restoration movement over the past forty years. He was a Founder Member of the Old Gaffers Association, and the President of the OGA in the 1980s. He has a cottage in East Looe.

Cover: Front The *Reliance* off East Looe. **Back** The *Guide Me* and the *Reliance* racing. {Author}

An elderly 'jouwster' at Newlyn with the Mount's Bay crab boat *Jenny* hauled up in an alley for protection.

Luggers leaving Looe in about 1907.

CONTENTS

Ocean Pride and *Snowball*

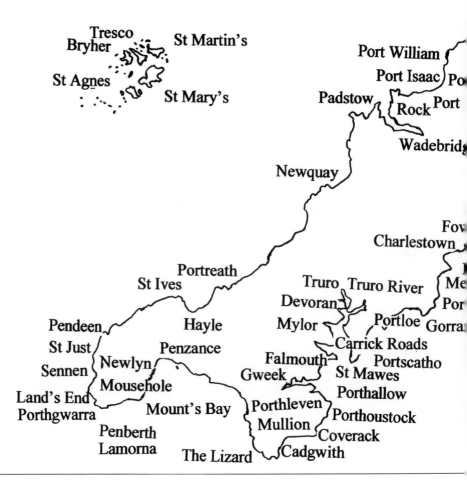

Lydn

Hartl

Marslan

The Isles of Scilly are about 28 miles south west of Land's End

Tresco — St Martin's
Bryher
St Agnes
St Mary's

Port William
Port Isaac / Po
Padstow, Rock Port
Wadebrid

Newquay

Fov
Charlestown

Portreath
St Ives
Truro Truro River Me
Devoran Por
Pendeen Hayle Mylor Portloe Gorra
St Just Carrick Roads
Sennen Newlyn Penzance Falmouth Portscatho
Mousehole Gweek St Mawes
Land's End Mount's Bay Porthallow
Porthgwarra Porthleven Porthoustock
Penberth Mullion Coverack
Lamorna The Lizard Cadgwith

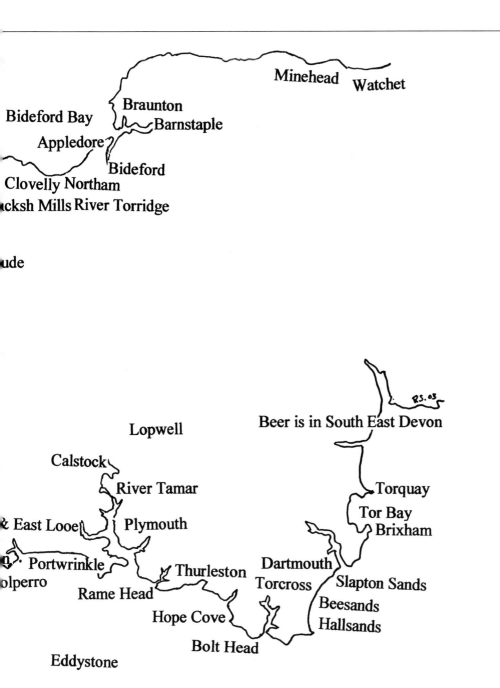

Minehead Watchet

Braunton

Bideford Bay

Barnstaple

Appledore

Bideford

Clovelly Northam

ıcksh Mills River Torridge

ıde

Lopwell

Beer is in South East Devon

R5.03

Calstock

River Tamar

Torquay

Tor Bay

East Looe

Plymouth

Brixham

Portwrinkle

Thurleston

Dartmouth

olperro

Rame Head

Torcross

Slapton Sands

Hope Cove

Beesands

Hallsands

Bolt Head

Eddystone

The Lugger Coast of the west of Britain.

ix

Peter Herbert on the *Agnes* 1955

Peter Herbert sweeping out the hold on *Agnes* in 1956.

A VIEW ACROSS THE BAY

An Introduction

From Padstow Bar to Lundy Light
It's a sailor's grave by day or night

The sea was calm, and there was not a single ship of any description moving, either toward Bideford Bar or up into the Bristol Channel in the blue waters of Bideford Bay. It was a clear September day and we had a wonderful view from the high ground at Northam across the green fields of north Devon. A century ago these waters would have been alive with small commercial craft. I was at Northam visiting Peter Herbert who, at the start of his long career at sea, had witnessed the very end of the age of sailing traders in the west.

Peter, a restless man always itching to get to sea, talked of his family at Bude where he had grown up overlooking the harbour. Grandfather *'Foxy'* Herbert (a nickname Peter inherited) had been a schooner captain and had become a first lifeguard on 'bathing patrol'. He had patrolled the beach in his heavy sailor's clothes and to make a rescue just kicked off his thigh boots and dashed into the sea fully clothed. The grandfather remembered the first surfers at Bude in 1911 who simply rode the waves ashore on a plank.

Just before World War II Peter went off pulling an oar in the hobbler's boat when they went out to pilot a craft in, or went on a salvaging trip. This boat, the *Alcide,* had come ashore from a Breton schooner at Stanbury Mouth about 1935. World War II saw a rich crop of wreckage ashore on the North Cornish coast. When something was found the wreckers' first trick was to remove all signs of identification. Then, if possible, to remove it before the Receiver of Wrecks claimed it!

In 1942 an open boat, probably the Captain's boat off a German ship, was washed ashore at Cleave Strand, St Gennys and was found by the Coastguard Russell Heard. He salvaged the boat

The 22ft *Tanya* at the Castle shipyard, Bude with Terry Heard, Guy Heard and Jannie Hamley in 1945.

and moved her up to Millook Beach. The Receiver of Wrecks said the boat was 'beyond repair' and sold her to Russell for £1. He then sold her to Guy Heard for £3 and he, and his brother Terry Heard, Hedley Hines and Peter Herbert took her back to Bude. This Captain's boat had a sail, but as there was no wind they rowed back in two hours. Here Guy converted her to a 'yacht' and named her *Tanya,* after a girl sniper that Russian propaganda claimed had shot 150 Germans. 'The sort of woman that every man dreamt of'!

The ketch *Traly* grounded at Bude with 'Flanders' Jewell sitting on his picarooner, 1939.

Peter had hoped to go to sea in a Bude vessel, but they had all given up by the time he went to sea. Michael Bouquet, that generous West Country author, said 'Bude was hard to enter and harder still to leave.' However just after World War II the shortage of tonnage meant that the Appledore motor sailing vessels were enjoying a brief and final revival. In 1949 Peter Herbert went as a 'boy' on the ketch *Progress,* but they still had a strong tradition of being run on a shoestring. One of his first jobs was to take the master, 'Granfer' Slade, his tea and six biscuits before sailing, at 6am. He repeated the task the next morning at Avonmouth but there were only two biscuits left. Slade was furious and demanded to know where the missing biscuits were. Peter explained that the mate, Billy Moyse, had eaten them. Slade was even more furious at the excessive consumption of biscuits. The crew sailed on a share of freight money and food, and after that Slade checked the packet daily to make sure that not too many were being eaten.

Peter Herbert was the last person examined by the Braunton Mutual Marine Shipowners Association. Being a master of a 'vessel', one of the little schooners and ketches trading over the Appledore Bar, was still a matter of tremendous local pride. But Peter thought a lot of people in North Devon got promoted to 'Captain' by the local paper. The lady freelance journalist who reported funerals got a halfpenny per word, so that by adding the word 'captain', twelve 'promotions' meant an extra six pence!

Bill Edwards, Tom Found (Harbourmaster), Walter Petherick (owner of the ketch *Ceres*), Alfie Petherick, Greener Marshall and Jan Darch (hobblers) on the sea lock at Bude in about 1934.

Above the fireplace in Peter's home at Northam was a painting of the motor trow *Emperor*, the first craft he became skipper of, when in 1951 he started trading with coal from Barry to Bridgwater. In 1955 he bought the little Bude ketch *Agnes* and traded her for two years. Although she was a motor sailor I suppose Peter was, by the time I met him, the last man around who had been captain of one of the Appledore trading ketches.

Peter had owned five of the Appledore ketches, went on to command numerous coasters and never lost a man or had a serious accident in his whole time as a ship's master. Also he never lost his great passion for buying up interesting commercial craft. Although it took a great deal of seamanship, his habit of operating the coasters single-handed was greatly disapproved of by the shore authorities. Once he bought the motor barge *Miller* at Cork and was preparing to sail for the Bristol Channel when the Harbour Master asked: 'You're not on your own down there?' Peter replied 'I have two hands aboard' meaning his left and his right.

On passage the *Miller*'s engine developed a fault and he put into Waterford. Just as he was ready to leave another Harbour Master asked the same question. Peter replied 'you don't think they would have let me leave Cork on my own do you!' The Harbour Master laughed and the *Miller* sailed safely on her way.

Another time Peter bought the Dutch coaster *Dispatch* and ran her from Barry to Bideford with 240 tons of coal. When his mate was away or in between getting crews he would operate her on the nine-hour passage by himself. One day the Harbour Master at Barry saw him running about the deck casting off ropes and asked where the crew was, but the *Dispatch* put to sea and headed down the Channel without giving a clear reply. It was not so much a career at sea as an adventure story.

When I left Peter he handed me a huge pile of photographs, the accumulation of a lifetime, and said 'there, I have written your book for you.' Not quite right, but his help has been a major contribution.

The same comment, and it was equally true, was made by Paul Greenwood when standing on the deck of the lugger *Our Boys* at East Looe. Looe has the second largest fishing fleet in Cornwall and fishermen call the berth above the Fish Market, where the luggers lie, 'dinosaur corner.' Here, between charter trips, the luggers *Deu Kerens, Our Daddy* and *Our Boys* are berthed.

A good catch of pilchards on a Mount's Bay lugger in about 1935.

The sailing luggers had gone decades before Paul Greenwood first went afloat, but his unique knowledge of the Cornish luggers came from listening to older fishermen talking. Paul started fishing from Looe in about 1962 as one of the six-man crew of the *IRIS*. Later he and Maggie bought the *Ibis,* a 42ft motor lugger built by Mitchell at Portmellon in 1930, and he used her for shark angling and mackerel fishing. In the mid-1970s the Scots purse seiners, after the herring fishery was closed to preserve stocks, turned to the Cornish mackerel fishery and trawling, sometimes supplying the Russian factory ships anchored in Falmouth Bay. This intensive purse seine netting decimated the Cornish mackerel shoals. At that time new faster trawlers, including the wooden ones built by Alan Toms at Polruan, made the older luggers unsuitable for commercial fishing so that in 1989 the *Ibis* was fitted with sails for charter trips. At the time Paul fitted sails on the *Ibis* he decided to restart the Looe Lugger Regatta and form the Cornish Lugger Association. This was the beginning of the revival of interest in the Cornish luggers.

Mike Darlington's dandy *Our Daddy* also berths near the bridge at Looe. Mike trained as a shipwright with Pope and Curtis' yard above the bridge up the West Looe River, but in 1965 he joined the five-man crew of the lugger *Our Daddy*. She was then skippered and owned by Alfred John 'AJ' Pengelly, born in 1906 and grandson of the original owner. The Looe fishermen found the name of this lugger a bit awkward so that she was always called *The Lord's Prayer* along the fish quay.

The 45ft dandy *Our Daddy,* racing in the Looe Lugger Regatta in 1995.

Dick Pearce had built *The Lord's Prayer* at Looe in 1921. During World War I there had been little fishing and stocks had increased so that the Pengellys, who had been working the lugger *Sweet Home,* wanted a large boat to land extra catches. Their new boat, *The Lord's Prayer,* was slightly larger than their old lugger, but was built with the lines of a sailing lugger. She carried a leg of mutton foresail and a mizzen, but was really a power craft with two engines, a 13hp and 7hp. The old fishermen hated to miss the free wind and to help power them home and save fuel they set the sails. When Mike Darlington started on *The Lord's Prayer* in the 1960s she still had sails, but they were never used.

This motor lugger was fishing mostly 'one tide' trips from Looe. Either south to Mount's Bay, or out east of the 'The Stone' (Eddystone Lighthouse). 'AJ' Pengelly was skipper and owner of *The Lord's Prayer* for sixty-five years and when he retired his son Terry and then Bill Wadling became skipper. After this the lugger was then taken to Plymouth where the hull was given a major rebuild and she was converted to a dandy rigged (gaff main and lug mizzen) yacht.

In 1985 Mike and Sue Darlington bought a 38ft fishing boat to run trips for visitors from Looe. This boat had been built by Payner at St Ives in 1920 as the *Our Florence.* Following the custom of the day this low-powered craft still carried a lugsail for use with a fair wind. Later this boat was fishing from Newlyn owned by two Spaniards, under the name *Dos Amigos.* It is considered bad luck to change the name of a boat, but the Darlingtons thought that if they just changed the name to the Cornish words for two friends, *Deu Kerens,* no harm would be done. In 2001 the *Deu Kerens* was sold, after sixteen years successfully running trips from the harbour, and Mike's dream came true when he, with his business partner Stuart Murray, bought the lugger *Our Daddy* and returned her to Looe for charter work.

When the *Our Daddy* goes up to her berth her masts are easily recognized over the rooftops from Lionel and Margaret Bowdler's house in East Looe. Their home looks across from East Looe to West Looe clinging to the steep side of the valley opposite. The river at Looe is very much a working harbour, but from the Bowdlers there is no sign of it. Just the masts of the fishing boats can be seen moving to and from the Fish Market. The Bowdlers can recognise most of the returning boats from their mast, particularly their own 41ft *Maret,* worked by their son Brian Bowdler.

The flood tide was seeping across the mud when we visited Ralph and Marie Bird beside Restronguet Creek. The yachtsmen give this creek a rather French pronounciation of Restronguet while the locals call it 'Strongwich.' Lower down the creek toward Carrick Roads, still exposed, was the Mine Bank. Back in the nineteenth century the returns from tin mining were so good that an artificial island was created in the middle of the creek and a mine-shaft sunk down to get at the tin. The miners worked away down the shaft even when the tide lapped around their island. Further up the creek at Devoran, schooners used to load materials from the mines and quarries from far inland. The quays have long since silted up and lower down the creek at Penpol, the Yard, which was the shipyard where William Ferris built the famous clipper schooner *Rhoda Mary* in 1868, is now built over with smart houses for those retreating to the serenity of Cornwall.

Ralph Bird's cottage overlooks Carnon Mill, a ruined building once used to extract tin from the Restronguet ooze that had been washed down from inland. Beside the cottage, in his workshop, Ralph was finishing off building his twenty-second Cornish gig for Newquay. When one considers that the gig *Newquay*, built in 1812, is still in the gig house at Newquay, how long will these equally beautiful modern gigs last?

Two decades before this we had travelled out to the Isles of Scilly just to see the gigs, of which there was then only a handful in existence. No traditional boat has made such a comeback as the Cornish gigs. Competitive rowing has given such community stimulation that gigs have spread far outside their native land.

During that same trip in 1981 we visited the north coast. Standing on a cliff overlooking Portgaverne, Pearl and I meet an elderly man. He told us how, when he was a young man, Port Isaac Bay was 'lit up like a town' at night when the great fleet of Cornish and East Coast drifters were out there laying their countless miles of nets. He also told us about the local lugger *Kindly Light* which had been caught out at sea in a gale and turned over when the fish in her hold shifted. The crew set out to swim to the shore leaving the

The 30ft gig *Sussex* was built in 1886 and rebuilt by Ralph Bird after she was blown over and smashed up in 1971.

Presumably it was blowing outside as this lugger was leaving St Ives under shortened sails.

skipper, who could not swim, clinging to the wreckage. When the gale dropped another lugger, the *Deerhound,* saw the gulls feeding on the herring of the wreck, sailed over and rescued the skipper. The other men reached the shore, but were later found dead from exposure on the open rocks.

Another local fishermen was suspected to have thrown a girl he 'got into trouble' over the cliff at the entrance to the cove at Portgaverne. The community, with its strong Methodist chapel creed of 'Right' and 'Wrong', saw the hand of divine justice when this man's boat upset coming ashore. He managed to swim ashore, but lost the boat and all his gear.

There had been fourteen open clinker boats at Portgaverne, but by the 1930s this era had passed and these boats, and the great seine boat, lay rotting in front of the pilchard cellars. We have been back to that spot since then and thought of the old lugger sailor and his memories. To him it really had been a golden age.

Today it is difficult to believe Portgaverne, and even Port Iaasc, were commercial ports, but just to the north there was an even more unlikely beach berth on Trebarwith Strand. Here a tiny patch of sand, sheltered by Dennis Point, was known as Port William. Ketches and trading smacks came ashore with coal from South Wales and left with slate from the Delaboles. It is doubtful if these beach berths were used much after the railway line reached this part of north Cornwall in 1894. It was just too time-consuming and dangerous.

This book is very much my own attempt to lift the veil of time and discover some of the everyday working practices of the age of sail. Whenever possible I have tried to get information first hand from the people who have lived it, but anyone tracing the history of the fishing industry in Britain has to acknowledge their debt to the books of Edgar J March. Although he only scratched the surface of the vast history of inshore fishing,

March, with his book *Sailing Drifters,* has stood in the background of anyone who has written about this subject. Not only did March start to gather facts just after the age of sail was dying, he also realised that photographs are the most reliable record of the past. Words and artwork are fascinating, but a photograph, providing it has not been altered, is the most accurate record. I have often searched for information and then realised that it is all there in front of me in some old photograph.

In 1983 John McDonald helped me with research for my book *Beach Boats of Britain,* some of which I have drawn on here. Finding the photographs is not easy and I have been greatly helped in Cornwall by Jenny Bennett of the Penryn-based magazine *Maritime, Life and Traditions.* Reg Watkiss of Penzance provided eight seine and luggers photographs, which was very generous, considering he is also an author of books on Cornwall. About a third of the photographs, particularly on north Cornwall and the Appledore ketches were taken or collected by Peter Herbert. Ralph Bird supplied seven photographs and some from the Isles of Scilly came from Gibsons. The majority were collected or have been taken by myself over several decades.

Alf Jenkins and Sara Powell have researched the Scillonian pilot cutters. Debbie Blackmore of the Polperro Harbour Trust read through the piece on that harbour while Charles Easterbrook and Malcolm Darch helped with the Devon Coast. When sailing on the *Vigilance* in Torbay Janet Cusack told us how, when this Brixham trawler returned home in 1997, after a gap of some sixty years, there was no one left in the town that remembered these craft sailing. It is difficult keeping these traditional craft to their working appearance after such a long break because people believe they are yachts. In the far west the great success of the racing gigs is that although there has been a massive revival, they have been kept to the traditional appearance.

Most of the people who have supplied the facts have been mentioned. Thanks also to Diana McMillan, my wife Pearl for undertaking the editing and son Jonathan for helping with the picture selection.

R.S.   Ramsholt.

Newlyn Pichards

Chapter One

BEACH BOATS

Beach Landings and Breakwater Harbours

Here is health to the Pope
And may he repent
And lengthen by six months
The term of lent
It always declared
Betwix the poles
There is nothing like pilchards
For saving the soul.

Pilchard Companies

It is one of those odd twists of fate that the staunchly Protestant coastal towns of Cornwall relied on fiercely Catholic Italy for their economic survival. From the Elizabethan period until just before World War I pilchards were the major fishery in Cornwall and South West Devon. Seine net fishing for pilchard appears to have started on the coast between Dartmouth and Looe and it was already organised in the Tudor period. The first record of exported salted pilchards was in 1555 when Queen Elizabeth's councillors wanted to stop the export of salted pilchards to 'the enemy' Spain. Although Spain was threatening to invade England, Elizabeth would not stop the trade. She knew it was the only income many Cornish towns had, and she needed the tax from it.

Before the mid-sixteenth century pilchards were smoked for export. The term 'fairmaids' salted pilchards came from the Spanish 'fumedos', meaning smoked, and this term continued to be used when salted fish came in.

Almost every cove and port between Portgaverne on the north coast and Dartmouth on the south coast had seine companies to harvest the pilchard shoals when they came inshore. At its height around 1870 there were 379 seine companies in Cornwall and a few more in southwest Devon. St Ives was the centre of this fishery and originally each company had a section of the coast they could operate in. However this led to disputes so that here, each company was given two days at a time when they could take any shoals that came inshore. The Companies used their large Tuck Boat, usually fitted with a sail, that would be anchored off and the men on look-out slept under the sail.

From July the pilchards arrived in the bays in vast shoals. Lookouts, known as 'huers', watched from 'Huers' Houses' on the cliff tops and when they saw the dark patch in the water of the shoals moving inshore, they signalled for the 'company' to go into action. Once the shoal was in a company's waters the men rowed out in three different types of boats. The smallest boat was used to direct the net laying. The net laying boats encircled the shoal and then it was dragged into the shore. Here the fish were loaded into the largest Tuck Boats and taken to the company's 'cellars' or 'palaces'. Once the net was dragged near the shore with the fish in it every able-bodied man, woman or child would turn out to take the fish out of the net and into the cellars where they were salted and stored in tanks before women packed them into the barrels. With a really big shoal this sometimes took days and they prayed for good weather so that the shoal was not lost.

The peak of the seine fishery was in 1871 when massive catches were made. Unfortunately many cellars ran out of salt and they marketed very poor quality pilchards so that many Italians were reluctant to buy Cornish pilchards after this. The seine companies also declined because the fish were being caught before they reached the coast, by the increasing number of luggers. All this activity led to serious over-fishing. There were around twenty companies at St Ives alone, and at one stage, to make matters worse, the Italians put a high tax on imported fish.

The largest catch of pilchards was 1,100 tons at St Ives in 1851. The second largest catch was landed at St Ives in 1905 when it took five tuck boats two days to get all the fish out of the net and ashore. By then seine netting was attracting the tourists and there were almost as many trippers out watching the seine net being emptied of fish as there were fishermen trying to ferry them ashore. The last time a seine net was used for pilchards was at St Ives in 1926, but the fishery had declined in most places long before this. Although over fishing did destroy the large shoals before they came inshore, there were still pilchards in the sea. Most of the Seine Companies gave up but the motor luggers still supplied the canneries. It was the demand for this fish that died out, rather than the fish themselves.

Some of the fishermen moved away in search of pilchard shoals. In north east Scotland on the Black Isle there are still Cornish surnames dating from the time when Cornish men moved up to Cromarty to continue pilchard fishing there, but for the most, the men developed different forms of fishing.

Pilot Gigs
In nautical terms gig was a usual term for a fast open rowing boat, but there were many different types in use all over the British Isles. The Cornish six-oared pilot gigs were light-weight, so that they could be carried up and down the beaches and their long narrow hulls allowed them to survive in the open seas. In Cornwall the gigs were mainly used for passenger work and racing. On the north coast racing four oared gigs was also very popular.

In the Isles of Scilly six-oared gigs were used for putting pilots off to ships and for salvaging on wrecks. There were also heavier gigs, such as *Sussex*, that were used for moving goods to the 'off islands' in Scilly.

Wayne Morris with the 1812 gig *Newquay*, oldest of the gigs, in Newquay gig house, 1988.

In the late eighteenth century until the 1820s smuggling in Cornwall was big business and good business. Some gigs were taken across to the Channel Islands or Brittany on smuggling trips. When the crew of the Revenue cutter spotted them the gigs escaped by being rowed up into the wind. As the sailing Revenue cutters were unable to catch the eight-oared gigs they were banned and only six-oared gigs were allowed. Richard Gillis, whose enthusiasm kept the Newquay gigs going, believed that the Peters family of St Mawes had developed the Cornish gigs in the late eighteenth century, although this type of open boat was probably far older in design.

The Scillions mainly used cutters for pilot work, but often towed a gig for the last dash to get to an incoming ship first. At sea, whenever possible, the gigs were sailed with a low dipping lug foresail. The Isles of Scilly gigs favoured a leg of mutton mizzen while the gigs on the Cornish mainland often had a small spritsail mizzen. The fishermen, after the gigs had finished, retained the mizzen. Worked their pots on neap tides and the mizzen helped to keep the bow up into the wind to make the boat steady. It also steadied the boat when returning in a big sea.

New Grimsby, Tresco, Isles of Scilly, 1981.

In the Isles of Scilly the boatmen often had a share in the gigs they were working. Piloting brought in an income, but it was salvaging that could bring rich rewards. The 31ft gig *Czar*, built by Peters in 1879 for boatmen on the Island of Bryher was intended to beat the rival pilot's gig *Golden Eagle*. The *Czar* paid for herself the day she arrived in the Isles of Scilly as she was towed by a steam yacht out to salvage two wrecks. In her centenary year *Czar* won the inter-island league race.

Last time a gig was used for pilot work was on December 21 1938, when the St Agnes gig *Gipsy* put the Trinity House pilot Jack Hicks aboard the *SS Foremost*. After this the

Old Grimsby gig houses, Tresco, Isles of Scilly, 1981.

Newquay gigs preparing to race from the Gannel to the Harbour in 1954. The *Slippen* just beat the *Dove.*

gigs were still used for inter-island work and occasional odd jobs. The gigs in Scilly were seldom left out on the open beaches because of the danger of being blown over and also because the freshwater rain would have rotted them. The air temperature in the thatched gig houses in Scilly also seems to have contributed to their longevity. The last time a gig was used in a rescue was in 1955 when the tramp steamer *Mando* ran on to Golden Bar in thick fog and was lost. The Bryher men launched the gig *Sussex*, which had not been in the water for twenty-six years, because she could be pulled amongst the rocks without having to worry about hitting them or getting seaweed caught around the prop. The lifeboat *Cunard* rescued the crew and the *Sussex* towed back the ship's lifeboat containing the crew's belongings.

The Newquay Rowing Club's gigs on the harbour beach in 1987. From left to right, *Newquay* (1812) *Dove* (1820) *Treffrey* (1838) *Active* (1974) *Good Intent* (1975) *Unity* (1978) *Speculation* (1988).

The Newquay Rowing Club continued to race gigs, although for long periods they left their gigs afloat in the harbour. In 1953 The Newquay Rowing Club sent a deputation out to the Isles of Scilly to purchase some of the gigs that the older men had kept stored in the gig houses. In 1962 the only gigs on Scilly were the *Czar*, *Sussex*, *Klondyke* and *Campernell* and when these were brought out for a race they leaked badly, but everyone was very keen on the event.

Tom Chudleigh with the gig *Czar* in Hugh Town, St Mary's, Scilly in 1981. He had built the *Serica* in this greenhouse.

Tom Chudleigh grew up on Tresco and after World War II when petrol was in short supply he and some other local men borrowed the gig *Bonnet* to row over to St Mary's. Later he moved to St Mary and started boat building. In 1967 he was commissioned to build the *Serica*, the first new gig in the twentieth century, and he built her on the 'good side' moulds of the 30ft *Bonnet*. The *Bonnet*, built by Peters in 1830, acquired her name through an old woman on St Martin's, believed to be a witch, who used to wave her bonnet to the gigs. The gig crews believed that this had increased their luck. The building of *Serica* was the beginning of the revival of interest in gig racing.

A party being taken out on the gig *Lloyd's* to see the wreck of the steamer *Earl of Arran* in the Isles of Scilly, 1872.

The first twentieth century gig built at Looe was the *Nornour* by Gerald Pearn, in 1971 for St Mary's, Isle of Scilly and in 1972 she was rowed to Roscoff. This was the first time a gig had been rowed to Brittany since the occasional smuggling trips in the 1890s. Jim Currah, who had been a shipwright at Pearns, built the gig *Ryder*, named after the town's old lifeboat, in 1992. Jim Currah and his son Dave have built most of their gigs in the buildings on the hilltop just above West Looe. It seems the *Speedwell* built for Rock in 2001 was their twenty-first gig. In 2003 they built the *Waterwitch* for Charlestown and Jim thought the one they were building for Saltash would be their twenty-sixth. Every one knows the Currah's workmanship was good, but their customers greatest point of discussion was the colour and the name of the new gig.

Ralph Bird of Devoran, pronounced 'Devrun', also works full time on building gigs. He bought the *Sussex* as a wreck and rebuilt her and in 1985 built his first new Cornish gig, the *Buller* for Cadgwith. The demand was so great, with new Rowing Clubs springing up all over Cornwall, that at one time he was building two new gigs a year, all with his trade mark, a thin rib in the bow and stern.

In Scilly, there are several surviving carrying gigs. Any size gig can be raced, but in Cornwall normally gigs built on the lines of *Treffry* are raced. The original 32ft gig *Treffry* was built by Peters at St Mawes in 1838 and is still owned by the Newquay Rowing Club. The original pilot gigs of the Isles of Scilly and Newquay are the oldest group of boats in the world that are still in regular use.

The St Martin's gig *Lily* setting out from St Martin's in 1905. Built by Peters for the St Martin's pilots, this gig was kept at the Old Quay.

The gig *Slippen* was used for training at St Mary's.

The practice of painting the gig's name on the bow goes back to the 1880s at least, but it became standard when racing became the chief purpose of the gigs. Having names on the bow made it more interesting for spectators. In the 1960s gig racing just took place at Newquay and on Scilly, but Clubs were gradually started all around Cornwall and Devon. This started slowly, Tom Chudleigh built early gigs that are named after the Newquay pilchard seine companies, but by the 1980s four new gigs were being built a year. In the 1990s it became a stampede so that by the end of the decade over a hundred gigs were being raced. By 2003, when twelve new gigs were under construction, there were clubs at Weymouth and Swanage and Ralph Bird was building a gig for St David's in West Wales.

The gig *Czar*, with Bill Jenkins as coxswain, with cattle alongside being swum ashore from the steamer Minnehaha at the back of Bryher, in 1910.

The annual World Gig Championship Races started in 1990. These keenly fought gig races are held over three days in the Isles of Scilly. The first race is from St Agnes and then a race over the mile and a half course between Nut Rock and St Mary's. The first year, nineteen gigs took part, but by 2002 eighty gig crews took part. Some two thousand rowers, coxswains and helpers went out to St Mary's. This caused major congestion afloat and stretched the island's accommodation facilities. When the World Championships started they just attracted teams from Cornwall and Devon, but by 2002 it had become a truly international event with teams from Holland, Australia, Massachusetts, France and the Faroe Islands.

For eight years the Caradon gig *Mary Newman* had won the men's competition, but in 2002 one club, Falmouth, won all three top prizes for the first time. The Falmouth men, in the borrowed gig *Irene*, beat the *Mary Newman* and the Rame's *Minnadhu*, while the Falmouth ladies gig, *Idas,* finished several lengths ahead of the Scillian *Tregarthen* to win the Ladies event. The Falmouth veterans also won with the *Idas*.

Rowing smaller boats is also popular in Cornwall. The Cornwall Rowing Association was founded in 1952 and by 2003 ten clubs belonged to it. They organise racing in the West of the Duchy, for carvel boats on the Truro River. These boats had been developed for racing from the dredging boats that are used for 'haul tow' oyster fishing on the Truro River, while in South East Cornwall the 18ft (5m5m) Flash boats are raced. These narrow four-oared boats derive from the clinker watermen's boats used in the nineteenth century.

The gig *Klondyke*, with *Czar's* sails, in the St Mary's Museum. The Klondyke was built in 1877 for the Coastguards, but did not have a name until the pilots on St Agnes bought her.

Clovelly, Cottages on Beach

Picarooners at Clovelly on the North Devon coast in about 1900.

Buck's Mills

A beach landing on Bideford Bay where the boats are hauled out of the water and stored beside the steep road leading up the cliff. There is an offshore sandbank that makes Buck's a difficult place to land. In the nineteenth century, when ketches and smacks brought hard coal from South Wales, donkeys took it up the track to the Lime Kiln. In 1976 the North Devon Museum Trust acquired the 11ft Clovelly ledger boat *Wave* at Buck's Mills. She still had a purple 'mourning line' painted around the hull, a West Country custom. Normally, on an owner's death, a boat at Buck's Mills would have been taken out and filled with stone until she sank, but the *Wave* escaped this fate.

'Long boom' smacks in the tiny harbour at Clovelly in about 1910.

Clovelly

Clovelly literally clings to the side of a cliff overlooking Bideford Bay. At the foot of Clovelly's steep cobble street is a stone pier that creates a small sheltered harbour. Back in the 1930s a Bude fisherman remarked to the Clovelly men 'us was windbound for the whole month of May,' and the Clovelly men all laughed. The brutal headland of Hartland Point shelters Bideford Bay from the prevailing south west wind and Clovelly men were able to go out while the huge ground swell on the open coast around the point had closed the harbour at Bude.

In the age of sail and oar the Clovelly men worked open carvel boats known as picarooners. The name came from the Spanish for 'sea-robbers' and these boats were chiefly used in the herring fishery. The picarooners mainly worked inshore and could get back into the harbour quicker than the Clovelly 'long boomed' smacks. Although the picarooners were all the same type, Jesse Dunn's *Rona* was the fastest under sail. These Clovelly boats were good seaboats and stones, off the beach, were used as ballast.

The 16ft Clovelly picarooner *Lady Edith* at Bude in about 1947.

Peter Herbert bought the picarooner *Lady Edith* in about 1947. She had been built at Appledore about ten years before and he intended to run pleasure trips from Bude. He went to the Appledore sailmaker 'Uncle Billy' Harris, told him the length of boat and they just made the sail with no further information. Peter also worked for the Harris' for ten shillings a day, which was good money, but they used to go in the pub at midday and when he had to buy 'Uncle Billy' a whiskey, it cost two shillings! Sailing the *Lady Edith*, a dipping lug, out of Bude was not a successful venture because he was very limited by the number of days he was able to go out to sea over the bar.

The picarooners dropped out of use at Clovelly, but a very heavily built boat from about 1931 is hanging up on display in the Clovelly Visitors Centre. The National Maritime Museum Cornwall, at Falmouth, has the *Little Mary*, a heavy 16ft picarooner that was probably built in the nineteenth century, while Tom Waters of Appledore has built the *Picaroon* on traditional lines.

Portgaverne

A cove here cuts into the rocks making a sheltered landing, except when the wind is in the west, when a huge swell funnels up the cove. The trading vessel *Prince Alfred* was rolled over by a gale here and pounded to pieces. But in one typical Victorian year 106 cargoes, mostly discharged by women, came in and the trader *Rifleman* came here until just before World War I. At that time there were thirteen boats fishing from Portgaverne and the pilchard cellars still survive.

John Harris at Clovelly in 1947 with his picarooner *Faith*. Bert Braund was walking up the beach behind.

Luggers hauled out at Port Isaac to be painted in about 1945.

Port Isaac

Port Isaac luggers were mainly used for herring and pilchard, while most modern boats are used for lobster potting. In the harbour the boats are moored on lines with their bows pointing towards the sea while the Fish Cellars have become fishermen's gear stores. When the Port Isaac sailing luggers were fitted with Brit engines their hulls were 'rose on' by making them a plank higher. This was common practice because the engines tended to pull the hulls down into the water. The sailing hulls were kept low because it made them easier to row. The Port Isaac men greatly favoured tarring their boats because they believed that tar flexed when the wooden hull moved. When the council tarred the road near the boats it was not unknown for a barrel to find its way into the fishermen's sheds.

Port Quin

Trading ketches used to come in to this tiny cove to deliver coal. There was pilchard and shell fishing from here, but it became a deserted village. According to a local tradition nearly all the men were lost in a storm in about 1890 and the women and children moved away, although it appears some families left for Canada when the local mine closed. The pilchard cellars were being converted to a private house in 1981.

Jim Honey with his boat *Dawn* at Port Isaac in 1947. The *Dawn* had been 'rose on', had an extra plank added to the sides, after the Brit engine was fitted.

Seine boats kept at Perranporth on the north coast of Cornwall.

Pendeen
Before 1914 there was a pilchard company at Pendeen and about a dozen boats fished from the Boat Cove. The boats were hauled up clear of the sea by a capstan and seaweed was used for the boats to run on. In the years between the two world wars the capstan bars broke and no one replaced them. Tom Trudgeon said the boats became increasingly heavier as they received another coat of tar each year, and the men got less inclined to haul them out. It was the classic case of boats wearing out, but they had not earned enough to buy replacements. Consequently everyone lost interest in inshore fishing.

In the nineteenth century the tin miners from Levant and Geevor Mines fished from the coves north of Whitesand Bay when there was little work. The fish were either sold to fellow miners or salted down for winter use. The miners used their skill with explosives to blast away rocks in the channel, but these coves were still very exposed when the wind was in the North-West and North. In 1982 seventy-five year old Tom Prudgeon, who had worked in the Geevor mine, remembered that the Pendeen men had luggers up to 21 ft long. They used to go about ten miles away down to the Longships, after gurnard, a red fish about a foot long. The smaller pulling boats often had trouble with the strong tides. If they failed to get into the cove, they were swept down to Sennen, about eight miles away. Weather conditions on the coast have not altered in the slightest over the years.

Around 1967 a village committee was formed to look after and develop the Boat Cove. By 1982 a new concrete slipway and huts had been built and a winch installed. Twelve boats, about half of them part timers, were fishing from the Boat Cove and a number of people wanted to keep boats here. Several of these were newcomers and their arrival caused a tremendous local row.

There was no public road, only a public footpath to the Boat Cove at Pendeen. This was not unusual because before the coming of cars men walked to and from work. Some considered it desirable that the more out of the way places around the British coast were free of tourists' cars. At Pendeen the farmer allowed the fishermen to use cars to get to the cove, but in 1982 this permission was withdrawn because of the increasing number of cars. The gateway used by the fishermen was blocked with stone. Six fishermen decided to go and remove the stones and the farmer's son tried to prevent them. A scuffle took place and he ended up in a pool of cow dung.

Priest's Cove
The men working in the Botallack Tin Mine, which closed in 1895, worked boats from Priest's Cove. It is said that the workings of Botallack were so close to the seabed that the men could hear pebbles moving around above them. In 1981 the men using the Priest's Cove on Cape Cornwall went out in open outboard boats which had to ride through huge rollers at the entrance.

Seine boat returning to Sennen in about 1898

A woodcut, of a St Ives seine boat rowing a net round a shoal of pilchards in about 1898.

THE FISHERMEN LIFTING THE FISH FROM THE NETS INTO THE BOATS BY MEANS OF BASKETS

HE PILCHARD-FISHING INDUSTRY AT ST IVE'S, CORNWALL

DRAWN BY J. NASH, R.I.

Woodcut of St Ives tuck boat empting a seine net.

Nick Howell in the Newlyn Pilchard Works with the 1904 presses.

Sennen Cove and The Cowloe rocks, 2003

Sennen Cove

The beach landings on the very tip of Cornwall are open to the full fury of the Atlantic, but none more so than Sennen Cove, just to the east of Land's End. Sennen is the first of the landings on the wild north coast and would not be there if it was not for the Cowloe. These rocks, thought to look like a cow when seen from the cliff top, slightly shelter this side of Whitesand Bay. There were eighty fishermen and eighteen boats working from Sennen Cove in 1850. These either went potting for crab or seine netting for pilchards and red mullet. The Sennen Cove luggers were about 20ft long and worked right out in the open Atlantic and sometimes went as far as The Scillies. Sometimes Sennen crabbers would lay on anchors in the Plo-an-ad, under shelter of the Cowloe, but in 1876 the Round House was built to house the capstan that had come from an old tin mine. After this the boats could be hauled up well clear of the seas. In 1908 Colonel H.W.Williams, MP for St Ives, raised the funds to build the granite breakwater that forms a slightly sheltered channel up to the beach landing, but in bad weather the seas break over the top of this wall.

Pilchards being discharged from a tuck boat at Sennen in about 1898.

Just to the south of Sennen Cove and Land's End are the Longships Rocks and in 1776 the first lighthouse was built on these rocks with material supplied from Sennen. For over two hundred years all the supplies for the Longships lighthouse were taken out from Sennen Cove. The main village of Sennen is on the cliff top, inland. The people from here are the 'Over Hillers' and in the past were quite separate from the fishing community of about one hundred people down near the cove.

Before World War I two-masted luggers used for crabbing worked from Sennen Cove and also undertook salvaging. Ocean-going ships coming in from the Atlantic at the end of a long voyage did not know their exact position and consequently were often unable to get clear of this inhospitable coast.

Salvaging from wrecks was not without its dangers, for in 1886 the Sennen luggers were returning deeply loaded from a wreck off Cornwall when a man was washed overboard from one of them, and was never seen again. However, a 'good wreck' was looked on as a godsend on the impoverished Cornish coast. A Swedish barque that was wrecked off Sennen in 1913 was remembered for decades afterwards with great affection because she had supplied all the cottages with household coal and firebricks for years.

Before World War I there were six seine companies working in Whitesand Bay for pilchards and some very large catches were made here, but the catches gradually got smaller. The 'huer's hut' on the cliff top fell down during World War I and when the men returned home from the fighting they did not revive the fishery. However the driving luggers were used for a few more years.

Although conditions around Land's End are very exposed the fishing is good. When Henry Hards started fishing from Sennen in 1949 he and his brother earned a good living working about fifty pots from the 25ft (7.62m) crabber *Henry & John*. In the 1960s there were still five large wooden boats working from the Cove, but by 1982 the five boats working from here were all below 19ft (5.79) long. Most of these, like the *Clair* that belonged to the lifeboat coxswain Morris Hutchinson, were GRP hulled.

In 2003 there were seven open boats on the landing, mainly potting in the summer. The problem with the landing is the huge groundswell, loved by the surfers, which is often started by a low-pressure storm hundreds of miles out in the Atlantic. The swell from these storms can suddenly arrive at the coast during fine weather.

Sometimes, huge shoals of mullet appeared in Whitesand Bay in March. The men of Sennen Cove turned out with special nets to harvest this rewarding crop. The exact amount of mullet landed from these shoals was a secret, closely guarded by the Sennen Covers. In 1982 the mullet had not appeared for three years, but some local people suggested that in the past a thousand stone (6.3 tonne) had been landed in one season and in a previous year four thousand stone (25 tonne) were taken.

The men of Sennen regard the mullet as being their property and literally fought off attempts by the men of St Just to join in. Once a French boat came inshore and tried to take the mullet, but they were driven off, by stoning. In about 1969 some men from Par decided to arrive by road with a boat and nets to go seine netting in Whitesand Bay. Spotting the arrival of the 'trespassers' about thirty Sennen men rushed down the hill armed with knives and stones. Faced with this aggressive opposition the Par men left, but promised to return in force. This they did, but as the two forces of very angry fishermen moved towards each other ready to do battle, the Penzance police, who had also arrived in force, got between them. The Par men were obliged to retire once more, empty-handed.

In 2003 the last remaining Cornish seine boat was a wreck in the corner of the car park behind the Sennen landing. A reminder of an industry that had once been very important to Cornwall.

Porthgwarra

The Atlantic swells roll in and hammer against miles of Cornish cliffs that line this most westerly part of the British mainland. There are a few places, on the twenty-five miles of coast between St Ives and Mousehole that boats can land and these are little more than clefts in the cliff. The fishermen working from the harbours have great respect for the 'Covers' who come riding in on the surf in their small open boats to these exposed landings.

The Porthgwarra landing, under the lee of Gwennap Head, is so small that it is hardly visible from the sea at high tide, but this cove is protected from every direction, but a southerly gale. The beach has been cleared of rocks to make a channel to the tiny landing slip. On one side, a man-made passage was cut through the rock by St Just miners, so that the horses and carts could collect seaweed for the farms. A Victorian watercolour of Porthgwarra showed eighteen open luggers hauled out. In the age of sail these would have often been rowed out to the Wolf Rock in search of fish.

In the autumn the men of Porthgwarra kept a constant watch for the pilchard shoals. In an age when most people lived on the edge of desperate poverty, the pilchard shoals were the only chance to make an income in cash. At night if the 'huer' spotted a dark patch in the water he set fire to the gorse as a sign that the shoal had arrived. Although only about eight men went out in seine boats, the whole district helped to get the catch into the cellars. All this stopped in 1916 when the seine boats landed their last pilchard shoal at Porthgwarra.

For several decades after this the lucrative lobster fishing around the Runnel Stone supported Porthgwarra fishermen. The last full-time fisherman living at Porthgwarra was Dick Rawlings, who retired in about 1967. In 1983 only four boats were kept there on the granite ramp, of which *Our Maggie* and *Snow Goose* were fished part-time while Mrs Rawlings acted as harbour master for the St Aubyn Estate. In the spring of 2003 there were only two dinghies above the very steep landing ramp.

Penberth

In the Victorian period the men of Penberth Cove fished in the summer and then became farmers, chiefly growing spring flowers. Between 1861-73 the Jackson Brothers worked the 48ft mackerel driver *White Star,* but most of the Penberth crabbing luggers were under 20ft long. The parson and squire owned the 24ft Penberth seine boat and because they had a financial stake in pilchard fishing, the squire ordered that no lobster pots were to be set in the Cove after the end of August. This resulted in a major local row between the seine company and the Jackson family who were lobster fishermen. In the end the Jacksons moved to Porthgwarra and the Chapples moved into the empty cottages at Penberth.

In 1983 seventy-three year old John Henry Chapple talked of seeing the Penberth Cove men 'shooting' a seine net for pilchard. The shoal they got was so large that the Porthgwarra seine boat also came to help and it took three days to empty the net. In the end the weather broke and the rest of the catch was lost. However, John Henry took £90 for his share, which was more than he earned for the rest of the year.

The Penberth crabbing luggers were hauled ashore by a huge wooden capstan suspended on a 24ft beam between two stone pillars. Following the normal Cornish practice the landowner owned the capstans but manning and maintaining them was a co-operative effort by the fishermen. This worked fine when there were about fifteen men fishing from the Cove and there were always enough 'bodies' to man the capstan. When Dave Chapple started full time fishing there were not enough men and it sometimes took half an hour to get his 17ft (5.18m) *Tunny PZ 145* up the slip. He first 'jigged in the water' for mackerel in about 1946, using a set of hooked feathers. The fishermen at Penberth were very pleased when the Penzance dentist Dave Motton, who kept a small boat here and loved this tranquil place, fitted a motor capstan in 1950. The *Tunny*, a wooden boat built by George Peaks at Newlyn in 1936, was used for potting and long lining from Penberth for just over sixty years.

The National Trust acquired Penberth Cove in 1957 and shortly after this men started doing really well at mackerel fishing. In 1959 the Penberth Winch Society was formed and for a time ran its own lorry. By the mid 1960s Penberth Cove had been placed in the top ten mackerel landing ports, all achieved by only a dozen men. Their success did not go un-noticed and before long the big purse seiners moved into this section of the coast.

A ladies crew rowing the new Truro gig *Royal,* built by Ralph Bird, in Carrick Roads, 1988.

In 1986 there were twelve men working twelve 16ft boats from the Cove. It is an incredibly difficult place to land. In the winter, coming back from bass or pollack fishing, the men wait just outside the breaking water counting the seas. About every seventh wave is a very large one and the men then put their boats just behind the breaking crest and ride in at speed with the spray flying up from the rocks around them. Landing calls for the co-operation of all the men to get the boats hauled up the paved foreshore quickly. For these small fishing communities to survive the men have to co-operate and they jointly own a seine net for grey mullet. Just as in the days of the old pilchard fishery, a 'huer' on the shore directs the operation, but he now keeps in touch with the boats by radio.

Lamorna

At Lamorna Cove, the first cove west of the Mousehole harbour a stone pier protects the sandy beach. This was built in 1854, so that ships could come in to load blocks of granite. There were three large quarries here from which the stone blocks were dragged down to the quay in chains. For the Great Exhibition of 1851 a 24ft high 20 ton stone was shipped from Lamorna to London. Stone from here was taken to build the Bishops, the Longships and Wolf Rock lighthouses and to build the Admiralty Pier at Dover and New Scotland Yard in London. Before the quarries closed in about 1911 it was found to be easier to ship the stone out of Penzance. As well as the quarries, Lamorna was also an active fishing cove, and local boats still take out fishing parties.

The 27ft St Michael's Mount barge. When restored she was given the very square lugsails of the eighteenth century.

St Michael's Mount

The Harbour on The Mount had been an important trading place until Penzance harbour was developed for the export of tin and copper. By 1481 The Mount had its own fish cellars and nine fishermen's cottages. In 1679 The Mount became the home of the St Aubyn family and they built the first harbour in 1727 and completed it in 1824. When The Mount was a successful port in the eighteenth century there was a population of around three hundred people, but most of them moved away in the mid-nineteenth century.

Although the National Trust owns St Michael's Mount, Lord St Levan, head of the St Aubyn family, lives there and owns the St Michael's Mount barge. This barge, with its liveried boatmen, was used as a ferry for the St Aubyns to get to the mainland when the Causeway was covered by the tide. This 27ft x 7ft, six-oared barge, an open clinker launch, was built in about 1790 on The Mount of elm planks steamed on to oak timbers and fastened by hand-cut diamond shaped roves. The barge also has a very square-cut eighteenth century lug foresail and standing lug mizzen.

In 1840 the barge was used as the ferry when Queen Victoria visited St Michael's and remained in use, with a second barge built in about 1820, until 1900 when they were left in a boathouse. In 1993 the Mount barge was restored. Stephen Mathews has worked as a boatman at St Michael's Mount and has been involved with the barge for several years. She does occasional trips but usually lies in the harbour on display for visitors. This barge is the oldest surviving Cornish lugger and very possibly the oldest boat afloat in the British Isles.

Luggers at Mullion's cove before the harbour was built.

Mullion

At Mullion the tremendous Atlantic swell comes boiling into the cove when the wind is in the south. In 1839 Mullion Cove's fishing fleet was anchored off the beach where a sudden gale wrecked all of them before they could be got ashore. A breakwater was built at the expense of Viscount Clifton in 1887, but even after the harbour wall had been built the boats were still hauled out to prevent them being smashed up by the swell. This piece of coast, from the Victorian fishermen's viewpoint, seems to have been good for wrecks. In the 1870s there was an average of one wreck a year to be salvaged, but there was a bad patch of seine netting between 1859 and 1864 when no pilchards were landed.

Eddie Munday of Mullion recalled that before World War I there were five pilchard seine companies operating from the cove. The local companies had a lookout 'huer' stationed on Mullion Island watching for the dark patches of the pilchard shoals approaching across the sandy bottom. Another sign was if the lookout saw any of the Mounts Bay drivers, luggers from Newlyn, start to lay out nets. However if the Mullion seine companies had a good catch they hired luggers to take them across to the market at Newlyn. Most of the pilchards were brought back to the curing cellar at Mullion (now a private house) where the oil was extracted as the fish were salted.

The last 'shoot'(casting the net) at Mullion was in 1921, almost the last time this was done in Cornwall. After this, lobstering and crabbing were the mainstay for Mullion fishermen. In 1983 there were five boats working from Mullion, but with seas rolling into the cove it is a very dangerous place to work a boat from. John Pascoe of the *Patrice* said that the swell considerably limited the days that they could safely put to sea.

The Lizard

There are the remains of pilchard cellars at Church Cove (Landewednack), almost on the end of the Lizard, with a winch for hauling boats up the very steep slipway. The reserve Lizard lifeboat was kept here and used when it was impossible to launch a boat at Polpeor Cove, just to the west of Lizard Point.

In 1982 fifteen boats were being worked from the tiny slip in Polpeor Cove, down at the end of the Lizard, the most southern point in Britain. Of these boats only four men were full-time fishing. The main fishing was netting for ray, turbot and round fish and lining for conger, ling and pollack. John Marshall, owner of the *Margaret*, used a small boat with an outboard for bass because 'the diesel frightened them over the rough ground.'

Cadgwith

One of the most active Cornish beach landings is Cadgwith, a sheltered cove under the lee of the Lizard. In the nineteenth century there was a seine company here. Most of the old pilchard cellars have been altered greatly, but 'Shanky's Café' at Cadgwith remains near to the original appearance.

In about 1980 Terry Ellis decided to make a seine net for grey mullet. Knowing mullet like to escape through a hole, he included a hole that led to another net. A lookout was kept on the cliff, just like in the old pilchard days, to watch the water to see when a shoal was approaching. A 30ft seine boat was used, launched with oars in place. The best of the early catch seems to have been 12 tons of mullet and two tons of grey mullet was often taken.

In 1982 there were ten modern grp hull boats working from the Cadgwith landing,

Cadgwith with seine boat.

mostly with forward wheel-shelters. The change to grp hulls took place in Cornwall quicker than in most places in Britain, partly because of the very hard conditions and also because of better returns from fishing. In 1987 there were sixteen men working eight boats, potting, tangle and gill netting, off the beach here. In the winter, when it becomes impossible to land at Cadgwith for weeks, some boats move to the Helford River and work from there.

In 2001 Cadgwith fisherman Nigel Legge was one of the few people still making the traditional Cornish hand-weave willow lobster pots. In the past, every cove and indeed almost every fisherman, wove pots in the winter, in their own style of 'inkwell' lobster pot. For instance the ones in the Isles of Scilly had tamarisk, not willow, bottoms. The willow pots only lasted one season and are now often sold as decorations, while the modern plastic Scottish creel pots will last up to eight years.

Nigel Legge has his willow supplied from Somerset, arriving in November when the wood is still green and easier to work. In the summer, when he takes out visitors on his trips to the pots, he uses modern plastic ones. The pots are baited with salted mackerel and from his 200 pots he hopes to get fifteen lobsters and on a good day twenty-five.

Coverack

An attractive fishing harbour on The Lizard. There was an attempt to build a lighhouse in 1570, but there was opposition because it was said this would draw pirates to a safe landing and deprive the Lords of the Manor from their rights to the wrecks. The 'Paris Hotel' gets its name from the 10,669 ton American liner *Paris*, which was run on the Lowland Point at full speed one night in May 1899. All the passengers were taken off safely and the liner eventually refloated, only to be lost, as the *Philadelphia*, on Rame Head in 1914. In 1985 the former pilchard cellars were still overlooking the stone pier and four 24ft boats were full-time fishing. Potting in the summer and gill netting in the winter.

Porthoustock

Porthoustock, pronouced 'Proustock', is a fishing cove on the Lizard peninsula. In the nineteenth century Porthoustock was dominated by the West of England Roadstone Co's stone quarries. Much of the cliff was quarried away and Falmouth sailing barges took the stone up to Tresillian for road-making.

The custom was for sailing ships to end their ocean voyages at Falmouth from where they would be towed to a port to discharge their cargoes. Ships 'closing the land' making for 'Falmouth for Orders' often finished on the rocky coast even after they had rounded the Lizard and were within sight of the harbour. Many finished up on the Manacles, an outcrop of rocks off the Manacle Point. Here bodies were collected after the liner *Mohegan* was wrecked on the Manacles in 1898. She sank in twenty minutes with the loss of 106 lives. Porthoustock still has a few boats hauled out and is used by divers searching for wrecks in the strong tides off the Lizard

Porthallow

'The Five Pilchards' pub at Porthallow, a cove landing with cottages behind a sandy beach, has some of the fittings off the 4-masted barque *City of Panama* that was wrecked on Nare Point in a bad storm in 1891.

Portscatho

Portscatho, on the side of Gerrans Bay, sheltered in the prevailing southwest winds, was another typical community that used to depend on the seine fishery. There was no real harbour here, just a slipway leading down a beach on which boats lay on ropes fixed to the cliff foot and low water mark. The Great Blizzard of 1891 did tremendous damage here. The quays and houses on the sea front were damaged and several boats smashed.

Portloe

The seventeenth century 'Lugger Inn', now a smart hotel, overlooks a tiny cove at Portloe while the former homes of fishermen have mostly become holiday homes. In the past it was a different story because there was a thriving pilchard fishery here. Before World War I schooners came in to discharge on the open beach and over forty open boats worked from Portloe. Even in the 1930s there were still fourteen boats fishing from here, but as one local man put it 'that was before holiday lets and house sales to up-county folk' altered the local community. By 1983 the landing was chained off so that everyone had to pay to use it, but three boats were still used from here, potting and netting for ray and angling.

In 2001 there were three grp boats, which mainly went potting, hauled out at Portloe. In the winter gales the seas come raging into the narrow gap in the cliffs and wash right up the slipway so that the boats have to be pulled right up to the winch house. A fisherman here said that they sometimes, in bad weather, went six weeks without being able to launch the boats. There were also a few part-time fishing boats using the slipway and the owner of *Hartley's Herring* returned with a good catch of red mullet.

East and West Portholland

The hamlets of East and West Portholland are on coves at the foot of tall cliffs on Veryan Bay. This section of the eastern Cornish coast is sheltered except in a southernly gale when huge seas come roaring in to the tiny beaches. It does not look a very welcoming place to work a fishing boat from, but like most of the beach landings around the coast of Britain it did once have an active fishing fleet.

The limekiln at East Portholland is one of hundreds around the south-west coast of England which in the nineteenth century burnt lime to put on the acidic fields. The chalk was burnt in the kilns to create lime, which was then spread on the soil to produce better fertility. The use of lime was one of the major breakthroughs in improving yields from the tiny Cornish fields. To feed the kilns small sailing ships brought in coal from South Wales. This coal was also used for household fires.

In 1982 there had been no commercial fishing at Portholland within living memory, but the wide beach at Portholland East had a windlass for hauling up pleasure craft. At Portholland West one boat (FH 267) was hauled out, there was no commercial fishing either. One elderly local complained of the house-owners, that 'they are all land folks.'

In 2001 the owner of *Iminik* FY 837 said he was normally based at Charlestown, but every autumn he trailed his boat over to Portholland for a few weeks. He said Veryan Bay was very good because it 'was not on anyone's doorstep'. That is, the big boats from harbours to the west and east did not bother to steam all the way to Veryan Bay if they could get a good catch nearer their home port.

Also on Veryan Bay is the sandy beach-landing at Porthluney Cove in front of Caerhays Castle. Because of the difficulties of getting a boat across the wide area of sand it does not appear to have been used by fishing boats, but cargoes were regularly landed here. 'Porth' is the Cornish word for port, meaning a place where a ship could discharge her cargo. In the early twentieth century the Appledore and Braunton schooners came here and probably the last one was the ketch *Hobah* in 1937.

Gorran Haven

The landing at Gorran Haven is protected from the south and east winds by a stone pier. A pier was built at Gorran in the fifteenth century and it was rebuilt in 1822 and then straightened and rebuilt again in 1888. There is mention of a seine net fishery at Gorran in 1270, but it became known later as a crabbing centre. The harbour is safe except in an easterly above Force 5, when there can be a heavy groundswell and the boats are hauled out.

In the nineteenth century the Gorran Haven boats were carvel-built, but kept to the eighteenth century spritsail main and mizzen. The Pill family seem to have been the local boatbuilders and Dick Pill took over in about 1875. He is believed to have built the 17ft *Ellen* which was acquired in its old age by the Maritime Trust. Like the *Barnabas* she was restored and handed over to the Cornish Maritime Trust.

During the nineteenth century the Gorran boats worked well off the land, lobster potting, long-lining and drift-net fishing for mackerel and pilchard. The Cornish historian James Whetter stated with suitably local pride 'The crab boats of St Gorran Haven are superior to any of their kind in the county, perhaps the world.' Drifters from the East Coast would call in here to buy boats and Devon smacks, on the way to Ireland, called in to buy crab pots made of willow.

Just after the World War I there were forty-five men fishing from Gorran Haven and five new motor crab boats were built with fuller bows than the old sailing ones. One of these

The Gorran Haven crabbers lay sheltered in their tiny harbour during a storm.

was the *Cotswold*, built by Richard Pill and named after *HMS Cotswold* in which he had served during World War I. She had a mizzen to make hauling the gear easier and was going to have a lugsail, but a Brit engine was fitted instead. Another of these Gorran crabbers is the 19ft 6inch *Albion*, also built in 1921. Geoff Fox continues to work the *Cotswold* from Gorran more or less as a hobby, and Gordon Couch rebuilt the *Albion* here in 1999.

Polkerris
St Austell Bay offers some shelter from the prevailing south-westerlies and Polkerris on the eastern shore is one of the many small Cornish communities that had a successful and long established seine pilchard fishery. There was a 'seine house' here in 1590 and the Rashleighs of Menabilly, a house later famous as being the home of novelist Daphne Du Maurier, later owned the cellar here. In order to help the seine netting company they built the half-moon breakwater in 1775 to protect the sandy beach. By the 1870s the seine company was in decline and finished in just over a decade. Across the bay at Porthpean the story is much the same but the pilchard cellars were converted into the local sailing club.

Portwrinkle
After Looe the cliffs sweep east around Whitesand Bay, pronounced 'W'itsend Bay', to Rame Head and the entrance of Plymouth Sound. In the Victorian period open crabbing luggers worked off the sandy beach at Seaton. Just to the east there is a tiny cove at Downderry and in 2002 two boats was kept here in the summer for crabbing, which in bad weather went around into the harbour at Looe.

Portwrinkle has a tiny stone pier at the foot of a cliff with former pilchard cellars on the road above. In the sixteenth and seventeenth centuries there was a considerable centre of pilchard fishing at Portwrinkle. The pilchard supported its own cooperage making barrels and the harbour had leading lights to show the entrance. A bad storm in 1882 destroyed much of the old pier. Seine netting died out first along this coast, but the fish were still there. In 1980 Looe boats "pair trawling" landed up to 40 tonnes of pilchards a day.

Portwrinkle caught the national headlines in February 2002 when the Maltese freighter *Kodima* ran ashore in a gale. The crew were all safely taken off and later the ship was towed away, but some 5000 tonnes of good quality pine, bound for Libya, went over the side. The foreshore at Whitesand Bay was covered in timber, but in spite of the best efforts of the police and the Receiver of Wrecks, cars and vans arrived from far and wide and within forty-eight hours most of the vast quantity of planks had just vanished.

Bigbury Bay
The rights to the pilchard fishery in Bigbury appear to have gone right back to the medieval period when they belonged to Buckfast Abbey. At Bigbury-on-Sea there are the remains, exposed at half tide, of the Huer's Hut, from where a look-out was kept for the pilchard shoals. Nearby is the 'Pilchard Inn' that dates back to the fourteenth century.

Hope Cove
Although a breakwater was built at Hope Cove in 1924, it is still a very exposed landing in south-west and north-west winds and the boats have to be pulled up clear of seas. When John Jarvis, the last man fishing full-time at Hope Cove, started in 1952 there were eleven boats working from here. Some one-man boats, but the largest was a 30-footer with a crew of three. The men 'could get a living' working within three miles of the Cove. Hope Cove boats were wooden and John Jarvis had his 27ft *Girl Jean II* built at Weymouth in 1981. By the time he retired in 2003 Jarvis was working up to six miles offshore and using six times the amount of gear used in 1952 to land the same amount of fish.

Younger men tried working fibreglass dories from Hope Cove, but it proved easier to base the boats in Salcombe. Several small open boats work along the shore for crabs, while the larger steel Salcombe crabbers work right out into the middle of The Channel.

Hallsands
The stone fishing village of Hallsands is famous for no longer existing. The fishermen of Lannacombe, a small landing just to the west of Start Point, worked alongside the fisher-men of Hallsands, just over the hill in Start Bay. In spite of their names, most of the landings on Start Bay have shingle beaches, perhaps the sands of former times have been erod-ed away. In the 1880s Hallsands and neighbouring Beesands men trained Labrador dogs to swim out to the returning boats, seize a piece of wood with a light line attached and return to the beach so that a heavy rope could be hauled ashore and the boat dragged up the beach stern first. Hallsands was a major crab fishery and the boats used were about 15ft long, a deep hull with spritsail main and a headsail.

In the 1880s well smacks from the Hamble River, which went on buying trips along the Irish and Cornish coasts, used to call in here to buy lobster, crab and a few crayfish. The smacks anchored and hoisted a red ensign to show they were ready to start buying. The Hallsands men then went out to their kegs (store pots) and took their catches over to the smacks. The crabs were tipped up on to the smack's deck from bushel baskets and the men moved around the boats walking on the crabs and not worrying about the crunching sound. Once all the Hallsands crabs were down in the wet well, which kept them alive, the smacks up-anchored and moved on to Beesands to load there.

In the 1890s 650,000 tons of gravel was dredged from the seabed in front of Hallsands to be used in the construction of the Devonport Royal Navy Dockyard. The fishermen protested about this, but they could not stop the dredging. By the time the dredging ceased in 1901 the beach level at Hallsands had dropped by seven feet and the sea encroached inland. The village's natural protection had been removed and in an easterly gale and the very high tide in 1917 some twenty-nine houses, the homes of about a hundred people, slipped into the sea in one day. In 1924 some of villagers were re-housed in North Hallsands, a hamlet overlooking the beach. In 2003 at North Hallsands there was still a hand winch sunk into the shingle and a group of angling boats.

The shingle street in front Beesands, south Devon in 1935.

Beesands

A single row of fishermen's thatched cottages used to overlook the shingle road and a wide shingle beach. In the Victorian period there were some twenty-eight 15ft and 22ft crab boats, and thirteen 17ft seine boats, all clinker built, at Beesands. The seine boats were doubled-ended and were rowed. These were mainly used for summer fishing and in the winter men either dredged oysters or worked on the land.

In the 1950s the Beesands motorboats were high-sided clinker boats varnished in the South Coast manner. The beach has eroded away and large boulders have been placed along the beach to protect the village. In 1996 Britannia Shellfish was started, just behind Beesands beach. Several men went crabbing part time in the summer, but by 2003 there was only one full-time fisherman, Fred Hutchings, crabbing from here with a 19ft Fast Boat. In the winter he works his boat out of Dartmouth. Any conger eels caught are hung up to dry and used as bait during the summer.

Torcross

The seafront houses on Start Bay at Torcross sit on a shingle ridge between the beach and a mere known as Slapton Ley. The concrete sea wall was built in 1980 after the village was badly damaged in a winter gale.

Before World War I, Lannacombe, Hallsands, Beesands and Slapton Sands were collectively referred to as the Torcross landing. In 1863 Torcross had three seine boats, six mackerel seine boats, six pilchard drifting boats and about a dozen crab boats.

Slapton Sands

This was a beach landing below the main village of Slapton, at the eastern end of Slapton Ley. In 1934 Austin Farrar, an apprentice at a Dartmouth shipyard, cycled over to Slapton Sands to look at the seine boats kept on the beach and being used regularly. These beamy 24ft double-ended clinker boats were rowed by four men and had a 'deck' in the stern for the net to be flaked down on. The boats were light enough for the men to pull them up the beach with a hand winch. The men had a lookout station on the clifftop to spot the shoals in the Bay. Salmon was the most profitable catch, but they also landed mackerel and mullet.

Alan Abbot's *Sea Witch* at Beer with a three masted rig in 1986. As this was not really practical for the Beer Lugger Club's Monday evening races, she was usually sailed with two masts.

At this time Mr Lidstone of Dartmouth, who always wore a bowler hat, and his son Phil, built a new seine boat for Slapton Sands which replaced the boat that had been built by Mr Lidstone and his father about twenty-five years before. The fishermen wanted a boat a bit finer in the stern, so the Lidstones went over to Slapton by bus, looked at the boats on the beach, and with just a single mould brought down from a nail on the wall, built the new Start Bay seine boat.

During World War II Slapton was evacuated while the beach became a battle training area. Training took place here for the Normandy Landing and Start Bay was the scene of heavy loss of life when German E-Boats sank a number of landing craft that were out on a practice run.

The 'long sheets' for hauling the foresail around the mast can be seen on this lugger, which was racing at Beer in 1987.

Beer

Beer became famous in nautical circles because it was the last place in the British Isles to have three-masted luggers. The steep shingle beach at Beer is protected from the prevailing south-westerly winds by the 426ft high Beer Head. The village has long been a fishing centre and it was claimed that 'Beer made Brixham, Brixham made the North Sea.' This piece of folklore suggests that trawling was invented at Beer, and was then adopted by Brixham smacks that went on to trawl in the North Sea.

By 1900 the Beer trawlers were open, high-sided clinker luggers of about 28ft. The magnificent Washbourne Memorial Fisherman's Capstan, at the bottom of Sea Hill, is a reminder of the daily difficulties of getting large boats ashore. For drifting, the Beer boats operated as two-masted luggers, but when more power was needed to tow a trawl they stepped a mainmast amidships. The three-masted Beer luggers raced in local regattas until 1914. When fish prices rose, at the start of World War I, the Beer boat *Little Jim* was fitted with a Brit engine. Over the next two years all the large Beer boats were fitted with engines. The last three-master trawling was the *Beatrice Annie* in 1917. The last surviving three-master was the *Sapphire*, which was broken up in 1935.

In 1984 Alan Abbott whose father and grandfather had been Beer fishermen, decided to rig out the 17ft *Sea Witch* as a three-masted lugger. This aroused great interest at Beer and led on to start the Monday evening races. None of the original Beer luggers had survived, but the small clinker boats were still used on the beach and these were rigged out with sails. The old Beer luggers had a single sheet and swung the sail around forward, when tacking. It was a short step on from this for Beer racing boats to be fitted with 'long sheets' to pull the sail around to the leeward side. This easier way of tacking made the luggers more acceptable to racing men although it does wear the leading edge of the sail. The relentless enthusiasm for racing at Beer has resulted in a new type of day racing boat appearing. New wooden Beer luggers are the 16.7ft *Moondance* built in 2002 and in 2003 the *Enterprise* joined the fleet. These remained two-masted luggers with the characteristic long iron bumkins on the bow tilted downwards.

Beer luggers racing in 1987. The *Sunshine* on the right has a cabin.

Liveried boatmen on the St Michael's Mount barge.

Jim Currah, and his grandson, building the gig *Speedwell,* at West Looe for Rock, 2001.

Ralph Bird with a new gig for Newquay at Devoran, 2003.

The Men's Group in the first World Pilot Gig Championships in the Isles of Scilly, 1990.

The gig *Irene* rowed by the Falmouth Gig Club won the 2002 World Gig Championship in Scilly, 2002.

The St Ives gig *Porthminster*, built by Peter Foord in 1992, at the Portsmouth Festival of the Sea, 2001.

The St Ives lugger *Dolly Pentreath* at St Ives.

Chapter Two

LUGGERS IN THE WEST

The Pilchard whose bodies yield the fragrant oil
And makes London's lamps Midnight smile.
Peter Pindar 1783

LUGGERS AND DRIFT NETTING

Before the eighteenth century the Cornish did not work far offshore, partly because there was enough fish inshore, but also because of pirates from the Barbary Coast raiding in search of slaves. The Cornish concentrated on the inshore seine fishery for pilchards, which was a successful commercial operation for the company owners, but individual fishermen began to seek the shoals further out to sea. Fishermen have boats built to suit the type of fishing they are engaged in. When the fishing methods change, the boats also change. In the Duchy of Cornwall, in the nineteenth century, driftnet fishing for shoals swimming near the surface became standard practice and the lugger was the type of boat most suited for this.

The boats began to work further out to sea and laid out about a mile of nets and then drifted with the tide through the night. The advantage of the two-masted lugger was that when the craft lay to its nets drifting, the foremast, a large mast in the bow could be lowered to the deck to reduce the strain on the hull. Also, with the mizzen set, the luggers would lay head to wind, making it slightly more comfortable for the crew trying to get some rest before hauling. Another advantage of the lugger was that sails could be lowered very quickly. This was essential when coming into the small Cornish harbours where space was limited and they had to be able to stop quickly. The great disadvantage with the dipping lug was that when sailing against the wind, the forelug (or foresail) had to be moved to the leeward side of the mast. Each time the craft came around on a fresh tack the sail had to be 'dipped' around to the opposite side. However, since handling driftnets required several hands there was adequate labour force available. Shifting the foresail at sea was problematic, in fact downright dangerous if you were not used to it, but the Cornish fishermen did it all their lives and became very good at it.

The lug rig probably evolved out of the medieval square sail. In order to sail closer to the wind the leading edge of the square sail was pulled up tight with a 'bowline.' This appears to have led on to the head of the square sail being cut at an angle, which created the lugsail that made the boat faster.

There was a tremendous financial incentive to produce a craft that could out sail the British Revenue Cutters. The luggers proved they could do this, partly because they were sometimes larger than the Revenue Cutters and the extra waterline length gave them more speed, but in the days of the loose woven sails and hemp rigging the smuggling luggers, with tackles on the halyards, could get their sails set up much tighter. This allowed them to sail closer to the wind, and often faster, than the gaff-rigged cutters of the Revenue Service. Because of the huge profits made from smuggling, and privateering, the English and French builders, watched each other very closely as they both had a strong incentive to produce the fastest vessel to make as much money as possible.

Some of the British three-masted smuggling luggers were very powerful craft. In Polperro, where smuggling was run almost as a legitimate business, the luggers included the 80ton *Swallow*, 102ton *Unity* and the 120ton *Brilliant*. The *Brilliant* had a crew of sixty, twelve carriage guns and six swivel guns. This lugger was running goods to the Cornish coasts for twenty years before she was finally seized in 1804. The smuggling luggers, in a fair breeze, were able to sail from Roscoff to Polperro in eight hours and the Revenue cutters could not even keep them in sight. No wonder the fishermen, many of whom were smugglers, became keen on luggers.

Newquay boats in the harbour in about 1935.

It is likely that the Cornish luggers actually evolved in Mount's Bay. In the seventeenth century open two-masted boats with square sails were used in the drift net fishery. In the early nineteenth century open clinker built three-masted luggers with very square lugsails were used. In about 1850 a lugger with a very high peaked lug came around from St Ives and won the Mount's Bay regatta. The Newlyn and Mousehole men quickly saw the advantage and produced luggers with an even higher cut sail. It appears that the early boats were clinker-built, in the Norse tradition, but contact with the French meant that carvel hulls became general throughout much of the West Country. There were few hard and fast rules with traditional workboat types. There were always some fishermen who would try something new and if it was a success then others quickly adopted the idea.

In 1859 the Royal Albert Bridge across the River Tamar gave Cornwall a rail link to the huge markets 'up country'. Fresh fish had always been hawked by 'jouwsters', fish sellers carrying their fish in baskets on their backs around the villages, but after the rail link was opened turbot, ray, conger and ling were sent, fresh, to the industrial towns. This new market greatly increased the number of boats working from the small harbours in the Duchy of Cornwall, but there was still a great deal of poverty in the fishing communities.

The early nineteenth century fishing luggers were open boats with round bluff bows and appear to have been fast. Once in 1854 some Newlyn fishermen were drinking in the 'Star' Tavern, opposite the Pilchard Works, and declared that they were fed up with fishing and would sail to take part in the Australian Gold Rush. In the lugger *Mystery*, decked over for the voyage, they sailed out to Melbourne in 116 days. This included a stop at Cape Town and had been faster that many of the square-rigged ships.

St Ives mackerel drivers at Tweedmouth, Berwick on Tweed with fifies from the Firth of Forth in the background in about 1910.

The Cornish boats were used to making voyages away from their home waters. By the eighteenth century they were going to the Isle of Man for part of the year. They also sailed to the mackerel spawning grounds of SW Ireland and worked from ports in Ireland. Because the Cornish boats were fast and handy the Isle of Man and Irish fishermen, who produced their own versions of the two-masted lugger, copied them. By the end of the nineteenth century fishermen in Sussex and East Anglia were also buying new boats from Cornish builders, particularly from Porthleven.

The fishermen lived in tiny cottages with large families and these conditions were mirrored afloat. The first Mevagissey lugger, the 32ft *Band of Hope,* sailed to the North Sea fishery in 1863 and her crew of four lived in the 7ft cuddy in the bow. Even the decked luggers forward cabins were very cramped with six men eating and sleeping on the long voyages to Ireland and the North Sea.

A Mount's Bay lugger at Whitby. The lugger 195 PZ is drying her mizzen and cotton drift nets are hung over the bow.

The sails on the luggers were being dried at St Ives about 1913 when there were 605 fishermen in the town. If the flax sails were not dried regularly they rotted.

Newlyn is credited with adopting the first fine bowed boats, in about 1865, and these were soon adopted at Mousehole and Porthleven. These boats were still open, which led to many being swamped in heavy seas, but around 1875, decked craft were built. Thus the classic Cornish luggers, of about 38-42ft long, were born. The Lizard was the divide between two types of luggers. Most of the sailing luggers from the small harbour west of the Lizard were 'double bowed', that is they had pointed sterns, so that when banging about in the harbours they did not damage their hulls. St Ives was very prone to a heavy groundswell rolling into the harbour, which meant that the luggers here were almost flat-bottomed and very strongly built. The East Cornish luggers, from east of the Lizard, were much finer lined and had transom sterns, sloping at Mevagissey and straight at Looe, but there were no hard and fast rules. The fishermen had to have a boat they could afford and every fisherman had his own idea of the perfect boat for the job.

The inshore seine fishermen called the luggers 'drivers' because they broke up the shoals before they could reach the coastal bays. The local businessmen and landowners controlled the seine pilchard companies and to protect their interests brought in by-laws to force the small pilchard 'drivers' to work further offshore. However the pilchard 'drivers' won this battle because they were cheaper to operate than the seine companies and they got to the shoals first.

Mousehole in about 1900. The men on the right are carrying down 'barked' drift nets to hang them over masts, to dry on the harbour wall. .

All Cornish luggers were tarred black until about 1910 when gradually brightly painted hulls became more popular. The crews in the sailing luggers owned some of the driftnets. Cotton nets were liable to rot if left in piles wet, and to try and preserve them they were 'barked', put into boiling 'cutch', a sap drawn from tree bark. Every task connected with fishing was done by hand labour and required a large number of people.

The fine lined mackerel 'drivers' that worked from Mount's Bay and St Ives went up to about eighty-a hundred miles out in to the open Atlantic. The Looe luggers went long lining 'out in the Channel' in the winter and were often caught by gales. If caught with the driftnets or long-lines down they would not cast this valuable gear adrift, but would ride it out. Often they would be driven away to 'The Wight' or down to Scilly. The only navigation aids were the compass and the skipper's uncanny knack of knowing where they were, but when the wind dropped they were often lost. This was normal, a steamer would be hailed, and once they had a position they went into the nearest port and sent a telegram home.

The *Twilight*, a Looe lugger built by Dick Pearce in 1900, was once on a day trip when her crew read the weather wrongly. The other Looe luggers thought it was the 'calm before the storm' and ran back to the harbour, but the *Twilight* carried on out, shot her gear and was then hit by a gale. Every day the families ashore watched the horizon, not knowing what had happened to her. But after a week the little group on the Banjo Pier watched *Twilight* come sailing slowly back round Looe Island.

The luggers carried three mizzens, the largest one for light weather had a jenny yard on the outhaul, to increase the sail area. For extreme conditions, a small 'kicker' of stout canvas was set. A mizzen sets much better if sheeted out to a really long 'mizzen boom.' The mizzen boom on a lugger is 'steeved' upwards to keep clear of the seas.

The lugger *Boy Joe* sailing hard in Mount's Bay in about 1905.

The Cornish lugger men did not like reefing their fore-lug in a blow. Instead, as the wind increased, the mizzen sail was shifted forward on to the foremast and a smaller mizzen set. The storm rig was the kicker set on the foremast and after that it was 'bare poles.' In light weather a mizzen topsail was set and sometimes for passage-making a mizzen staysail and jib on a 'borsp'(bowsprit). The real job of the jib was to sail downwind when laying out the driftnets.

Just before World War I, engines started to be fitted and then new 'luggers' appeared which were motor craft with sails that saved a bit of fuel when there was a fair wind. The motor luggers built up to World War II were very similar to the old sailing luggers, but had bluffer bows to give more deck space. Also the interwar luggers had less draught, since they didn't need a deep hull to grip the water and sail.

The first sailing lugger at Looe to have an engine fitted was Ness and Johnny Richard's *Undaunted*. She had a 7hp Kelvin petrol paraffin engine and used to charge six pence a time to tow the other luggers in and out of the river. The engines were so successful that within a few years no luggers were relying on sail alone. Some of the larger luggers, such as *Talisman* and *IRIS*, were fitted with three engines. They had two props on the port quarter and only one on the starboard side where the nets were handled. On the sailing luggers it was believed that if nets were hauled on the port side the Devil was brought aboard. This belief has been forgotten and the motor herring boats did on a calm day haul their nets over the port side and no one believed it would bring bad luck. However by custom Cornish netters and mackerel boats still haul their nets over the starboard side.

The sailing luggers had worked nine drift nets, each one being ninety fathoms (164.7 meters) long. The motor luggers, because they could motor up into the wind, worked eighteen to twenty-two drift nets, which meant that one boat could land the same amount of fish as two sailing luggers. Many people believed that the pilchard fishery declined just before World War I, because, instead of staying inshore, the luggers with motors could get about twenty-miles offshore and take more shoals.

The nets on the sailing luggers were hauled by hand, although some luggers had small hand winches to haul in the 'footlins' (footlines) a rope that ran along the foot of the net. The head rope was hauled by hand. The men 'let the boat do the work' and as the boat rolled they hauled in the slack and then jammed the head rope with their knee against the rail as the boats heaved up. A calm was the worst because it was then a dead haul.

The counter-stern motor drifter *Sheerness* in St Ives harbour.

When engines became available some fishermen tried new types of hulls. The basic hull remained the same but some added round 'Lowestoft drifter' counter sterns, similar to the *Sheerness*. During World War I the St Ives lugger *Mary Ann* was sunk by a German U-Boat and the crew were turned adrift in their punt. Some hours later *HMS Sheerness* picked up these survivors and took them into a Welsh port and they phoned home to say they were safe. When a replacement for the lost *Mary Ann* was built it was named *Sheerness* in honour of the Royal Navy ship that had saved them. The *Sheerness* worked from St Ives until 1969.

In 1968 I saw one of these counter-sterned boats in Padstow. This was the 55ft motor ketch *Mayflower of Camelot* that had been built by Dick Pearce in 1920, at West Looe, as a long-lining lugger. Another of these East Cornish counter-sterned luggers was the *Our Lizzie*. There were several of these built, but they were rather un-handy and were sold to Newlyn for long lining. Another new craft with a tugboat counter stern is the *Ocean Pride*, which was built by N.H.Peake & Sons at Newlyn in 1922. She was built as a dipping lugger with an auxiliary engine. The Broomfield brothers had ordered *Ocean Pride* as a mackerel and pilchard driver, but after the building had started the brothers fell out. She was going to be 50ft long, but the remaining brother had to economise and the lugger was shortened to 42ft, which is why she has a short bow.

At the same time as the *Mayflower* was being fitted out at Padstow, the 40ft Mevagissey lugger *Pride of the West*, a very old boat built of oak, was also rigged out for sailing, but as a yacht. Another Looe lugger to become a yacht, in 1936, was the *Guiding Star*, built by Angear at Looe in 1907 and she had been a winner at an Edwardian Looe Lugger Regatta. Later Brigadier Glennie and his wife owned her for thirty years and cruised all over Europe. These early conversions had all traces of a workboat removed. The *Guiding Star* became a dandy, fitted with a lug mizzen, and the gaff mainsail for easy handling when cruising. However, after the *Barnabas* restoration and the re-starting of the Looe Lugger Regatta in 1989, more people returned their boats to the traditional lug rig.

The 38ft lugger *Barnabas* at Falmouth, 1981. At the time she was being sailed without an engine by Terry Tuffery and Pat Crockford.

Over-fishing had become a problem that the European Economic Community was, if slightly clumsily, attempting to correct by reducing the number of boats fishing. Britain's interpretation of the Decommissioning rule was to saw up fishing boats. Since fishing boats, particularly the wooden ones, are as much apart of the character of an area as vernacular houses, this amounted to the destruction of regional culture. Even worse, it is very doubtful if it has done anything towards preserving fish stocks.

Looking under the jib boom of the schooner *Henrietta* towards the luggers lying in the Custom's House Quay, Falmouth. Commercial cargo vessels simply grew too large to get into these small harbours.

One of the Cornish boats which has been saved from this curious Government ruling is the *Lindy Lou* FY 382. She was saved by a Cornish photographer, Andrew Campbell, and used for running trips from Custom House Quay at Falmouth. The *Lindy Lou* had been built in 1947 by Curtis and Pape on the West Looe River for a private owner and was worked by Looe fishermen, long-lining and mackerel fishing. She was later sold to the Blamey brothers of Mevagissey who worked her until decommissioning in about 1998.

Pilchard and mackerel drivers leaving St Ives in 1904.

St Ives

In the nineteenth century St Ives, on the west coast of Cornwall, was the leading pilchard landing port, but it had a very exposed harbour. A gale sent huge seas rolling into the sandy bay. To try and give the boats some shelter the first stone pier was built in the fifteenth century. The engineer John Smeaton designed the Outer Pier in 1770 and throughout the Victorian period St Ives harbour was improved for the benefit of the growing fishing fleet.

St Ives, a Puritan stronghold long before John Wesley came to Cornwall to teach his Methodist gospels, banned Sunday fishing. This led to conflict when the East Coast luggers arrived and, although their crews also came from a strong chapel background, they did not have a tradition of 'No Sunday fishing.' In 1860 an East Coast lugger went into St Ives with mackerel caught over the weekend. There was a great row with the crew of a St Ives gig when asked to land them, which ended with the Cornishmen throwing the fish back into the sea. Again, in 1876, some East Coast luggers arrived on a Monday with a large catch taken on Sunday. The St Ives men, by shouting and making a disturbance, prevented an auction from taking place. The East Countrymen then set out to take their fish to Hayle, but St Ives men attacked them and tried to set fire to the carts. On this occasion they did get to Hayle by land, but the following year when fifty East Coast luggers appeared off St Ives ready to land their catch on Monday the crowd on the quay appeared so violent that they sailed straight to Hayle.

Launching the lugger *Unity*, built by Treorrows, at Porthgwidden Beach, St Ives in 1888. She was lost five years later.

Not all the St Ives crews abided by the chapel's 'No Sunday fishing' rule and in the winter of 1887 violence took place between different factions at St Ives. In 1896 there was a major riot at Newlyn, followed by a meeting at St Ives where it was declared that the harbour would continue to be 'Sabbath keepers' and any fish caught on a Sunday were not to be landed there. In fact the economics of fishing forced the Cornish boats to start to fish on Sunday nights, but until World War II most Cornish boats would not go to sea on a Sunday.

Around 1900 there were over ninety luggers owned in St Ives and fishermen painted the tops of their mizzen masts different colours so that they could recognise their craft. The mackerel fishing at St Ives lasted from February to June and after this, from the early seventeenth century, the boats went off to the Isle of Man and along the Irish coast. In about 1864 the first St Ives boats sailed to the North Sea herring fishery. These were open boats with the men just living under the forepeak. On the first voyage to the North Sea the luggers went via the Straits of Dover, but their later annual voyage was to sail up the Irish Sea, through the Firth and Forth Canal and the boats then started herring fishing at Berwick, and spent the summer and autumn following the shoals south. They returned through the Straits of Dover.

Luggers leaving St Ives with *Lucent* on the right in about 1902

Some St Ives boats from the sailing era eventually became yachts. One of these, built by S. Berryman on the St Ives beach in 1897 in six weeks, at the cost of £60, was later converted to the 34ft gaff yacht *Lucent* and voyaged to the Pacific. The dandy *Silvery Light*, built on the beach by W.R.Williams in 1884, still sails as a yacht.

Another surviving St Ives lugger is the *Barnabas,* built at St Ives as a mackerel driver in 1881 for Barnabas Thomas. She fished with an engine out of Falmouth and Newlyn until 1974 when the Maritime Trust converted her back to her original dipping lugger rig. This was the first Cornish lugger to be returned to sail and in 1994 her ownership was transferred to the Cornish Maritime Trust. In 1993 Norman Laity built the 34ft lugger *Dolly Pentreath*, on the lines of the St Ives mackerel driver *Godrevey*. She was the first Cornish lugger built for over sixty years and takes charter trips from St Ives.

Isles of Scilly

In the age of sail the Isles of Scilly were a graveyard for ships and men. With their limited navigational aids ships came in from Atlantic voyages not knowing their correct position. The most disastrous of these shipwrecks was in 1707, when Rear Admiral Sir Cloudesley Shovel was returning with a squadron of Royal Navy ships which had attacked the French at Toulon. A gale hit them and Shovel thought his squadron was heading for the English Channel, but in fact sailed into the outer reefs off the Isles of Scilly. In the darkness Shovel's 90-gun *Association* was wrecked on the Gilstone reef. All three ships were lost that night and over two hundred men drowned. According to local tradition Shovel had managed to get ashore, but was murdered on the beach at Porth Hellick, St Mary's, by a women who stole the jewels from his fingers.

The loss of the *Association* is the most famous shipwreck, but ships frequently found themselves on a lee shore and could not sail away from the land. In the mid-nineteenth century an average of over thirty people a year were drowned in shipwrecks in Scilly. A particularly tragic wreck was in 1875 when the transatlantic liner *Schiller* was wrecked with the loss of 322 lives.

The Scillonians concentrated on smuggling, salvaging and pilotage and left the fishing, until there was a reliable ferry to the mainland, to visiting boats from Cornwall and Brittany. It was claimed that when the drifters went into Hugh Town, St Mary's it was possible to walk on the decks of drifters, from the Quay right across the harbour to the Lifeboat slip. Steamers took the fish landed here to France. A large fleet of Breton boats went potting for crab and lobster on the Seven Stones and went into St Mary's where they were popular because it was said they spent more in a day that the Scotsmen spent in a year.

Over seventy Mount's Bay mackerel luggers anchored off Hugh Town, St Mary's, Isles of Scilly. After 1800 there were three seine net companies, Friendship, Habnab and Industry in Scilly.

The East Coast drifters' practice of fishing on Sunday led to a fist fight on the Quay at St Mary's between the men from Mousehole and Newlyn, all staunch Methodists, and the crews of the Yarmouth drifters. Dorrien Smith, Governor of the Isles of Scilly, faced with a possible riot, said that unless the fighting stopped he would not allow the drifters to land in St Mary's and this seemed to end the fighting, but not the bad feeling.

Mousehole

Mousehole, pronounced 'Mouzel', appears to have been the first major fishing port on Mount's Bay, but was later overshadowed by other harbours. Sheltered by St Clement's Isle, Mousehole is believed to be the first Cornish cove to be given a stone pier to create a harbour. The Spanish sacked the town in 1595. This first pier was built in 1266 and the last piece of the harbour wall was built in about 1868. By 1849 there were 425 fishermen employed in the luggers working from Mousehole. This created enough income for the original pier to be extended in 1840 and a second built in 1861. The *Betsey*, the last 3-masted Mousehole lugger, was still going to the North Sea herring fishery in about 1840, but by then three masters were being replaced by two masters.

After World War II facilities at Newlyn had improved so much that most of the Mount's Bay boats moved there. In the 1990s some 18ft 'punts' were supplying the Newlyn Pilchard Works and there was also is some potting in the summer. For much of the winter the harbour is closed by putting baulks of timber across the entrance to prevent the sand being washed out.

Luggers at Mousehole in about 1910.

Mousehole in about 1930 with a three-masted schooner being discharged and several luggers converted to motor craft The *Nellie Jane* PZ130 in the foreground has a fine sailing hull and 'legs' rigged to prevent her falling over at low tide.

Newlyn

Newlyn, tucked away in a sheltered corner of Mount's Bay, was well suited for landing fish and developed into Cornwall's leading fishing port. The first pier was built here in the fifteenth century and in the nineteenth century the harbour and quays were extended in 1866 and again 1873.

The arrival of the railway in the west was a tremendous benefit to the fishermen, but Penzance harbour proved difficult to enter. Instead drivers landed at Newlyn early on the tide and their catch was taken some two miles by horse and cart so that it could go on the 2pm train for Paddington.

A heavy rowing boat belonging to each lugger was kept at Newlyn. Usually 'yawlers', boys aged between ten and fourteen, manned these boats. As the lugger fleet returned the yawlers rowed off to meet their lugger. The yawlers threw their painter to the lugger as it sailed past and were pulled alongside. The skipper then went ashore in the boat with a bucket of fish to show the prospective buyers.

At Newlyn 'jouwsters', mostly women, bought fish from the luggers and then carried them around the district in a basket on their backs selling them from door to door. Mrs Norman Garstin, wife of one of the artists of the Newlyn School, used to buy fish from a jouwster and at Christmas time gave her an old petticoat. The next Christmas the jouwster pulled up her apron and with shrills of laughter showed her the brightly coloured petticoat from the year before. She was duly given another one.

Newlyn was sometimes called the 'mackerel metropolis'. Because it was improved, it attracted the fishermen of Lowestoft and the Cornish ports, to come and land here, but this

Fish being loaded into horse drawn carts at Newlyn, in about 1910.

led to problems with the East Coast men fishing on a Sunday. The Cornish were particularly bitter about Sunday fishing because when they went to Ireland, where the Catholic Church was all-powerful, they were not allowed to land fish caught on a Sunday.

The bitterness led to the Newlyn Riots of May 1896, a time when fish prices were low and the Sunday fishing really angered the Mount's Bay fishermen. The Lowestoft boats had returned to Newlyn, as they had done for several years, but on the evening of May 17 many Mousehole and Newlyn fishermen became very angry when they started to discharge fish. Next morning about three hundred Cornish fishermen, with their wives jeering them on in the background, arrived on the quay as an angry mob. The Coastguards made an attempt to prevent them boarding the Lowestoft drifters, but they were pushed aside and the Cornishmen boarded the East Coast boats and threw their fish into the harbour.

Some Lowestoft boats left the quay and put to sea, but the angry Cornish men followed in their luggers. Out in the Bay the Newlyn men succeeded in boarding eight Lowestoft boats and again threw their mackerel catch into the sea. They also slashed the sails and threw any moveable objects into the sea and hit any of the crews who tried to stop them. Then chains were put across the entrance to Newlyn harbour to prevent any Lowestoft boats entering.

Lowestoft Fishing fleet off Newlyn

Lowestoft drifters landing fish at Newlyn in about 1896. The fishermen moved around the coast of Britain following the shoals of fish.

Ashore, the Newlyn Magistrates did nothing to stop the Riot so the Cornishmen threw the portable wooden office of Hobson & Co of Lowestoft into the harbour. Several of the Lowestoft boats sailed across to Penzance and put in there. On Tuesday about three hundred men marched from Newlyn toward Penzance to smash up the Lowestoft boats, but this time the police, with a volunteer force of drifter men and dockers, met them on the sea front. A hand-to-hand fight took place and this time the Newlyn mob was driven back.

However, another group of Newlyn fishermen had put to sea in two luggers towing gigs. This time the Lowestoft drifters drove them off by throwing stones from their ballast. The Newlyn boats had to retreat back to their harbour and the Lowestoft boats sailed for Plymouth to discharge their fish.   On Thursday a destroyer and a gunboat with troops of the Berkshire Regiment arrived at Newlyn to take control.

Luggers at Newlyn in about 1909.

The St Ives lugger *Dolly Pentreath*.

Stephenson's wooden trawler *Excellent* on the slipway at Newlyn, 2002.

David Wakeley in the process of rebuilding Malcolm Mc Keand's pilot cutter *Kindly Light*, Gweek, 1999.

The *Three Sisters* approaching the Peak at Polperro harbour entrance.

An official enquiry was held, but no charge of criminal acts was made against the Cornishmen. Some of these fishermen however had to pay costs for the damage they had done. The enquiry ruled that there was no law preventing fish from being landed on any day of the week.

This was beginning of the decline of the great fleets of mackerel drivers because not long afterwards the East Coast steam drifters, attracted by the good harbour facilities at Newlyn, began to come down west. According to Edgar March, the last lugger operating under sail from Newlyn was the pilchard driver *Delhi* in 1921, barely a decade after the first engines were introduced. After 1921 a serious depression destroyed the markets and by 1930 there were only 34 motor fishing boats registered at Penzance.

St Ives luggers leaving Newlyn. This shows a capstan on the end of the pier that was used to haul sailing vessels in and out of the harbour.

Many of the houses in the waterside area of Newlyn were in poor condition and in the 1930s the Penzance Town Council decided to re-house the fishermen in a new estate at Gwavas. Many of the people of Newlyn hated this high-handed action, if well intended, and since they could not stop the local Council they got up a petition to put before Parliament. Over a thousand people signed the petition and it was delivered to London by the fishing boat *Rosebud*. Before the voyage a service was held in the Primitive Methodist chapel in Bosae Street and as they departed the quay was thronging with people singing 'Fight the Good Fight.'

In London the *Rosebud* was well received and a compromise was reached. The original clearance order had been to pull down 157 properties, but only one block came down and the rest were either repaired or in twenty-three cases left alone. The *Rosebud* ended her days rotting away at Lelant near St Ives.

Newlyn is the major fishing port in Cornwall and the trawlers operated by W.Stevenson & Son are the largest fleet under one ownership in Britain. Their oldest boat is the wooden *Excellent,* built by Forbes at Sandhaven 1930. The lugger *Children's Friend* at Newlyn was built in 1938 as the Scottish seiner *Sunbeam* and was converted to a lugger by W. Stevenson & Son to celebrate the first lugger their family had owned.

Newlyn in about 1900, with the 'double-bowed'(pointed sterned) luggers by the old pier.

Newlyn also has the last traditional Pilchard Works in Cornwall. In 1905 the Borzones of Genova started buying salted pilchards in casks from a cellar at Mevagissey and in 1927 the presses were moved to Newlyn. The works were closed when Nick Howell, who had been running a fresh fish retail business just up the road, bought it in 1981. Nick Howell then threw tremendous enthusiasm and management skills into reviving the Cornish pilchard industry. The Environmental Health Officers then banned the traditional method of salting as being 'unhealthy' because wooden boxes were being used. Airtight boxes were then used but this resulted in the next consignment of pilchards to G. Borzones turning out to be mouldy and un-saleable. The Environmental Health Officers reluctantly gave way and said rather begrudgingly, 'the whole place looks like a museum anyway.'

Nick Howell thought 'right, that's what we will do' and, with his Breton wife Marie-Therese, created an award-winning museum. The 1904 presses from Mevagissey are part of the museum on the second floor, while modern production is on the ground floor. In the 1990s 18ft 'punts' from Mousehole supplied the Works, but by 2002 six boats at Newlyn and Mevagissey were under contract to supply them.

Pilchards are now delivered in bins which can be handled by forklift trucks, while in the older cellars, fish were salted and stored in deep tanks for up to two years before being packed into casks or boxes. The Mousehole fishermen discovered that fish could be shaken from cotton nets far easier than from modern synthetic ones, when they used their forty year-old drift nets. Is seems that diamond-shaped mesh retains its shape.

Luggers leaving Newlyn. On the far left is one of the counter-stern luggers. A few of these were built on the south coast of Cornwall, but they were not very popular.

Penzance

The first stone pier was built here in the fifteenth century and the town grew to be the major trading port on Mount's Bay. Fishing boat owners moved away from this port, but the Mount's Bay Lugger Association of Penzance have saved the 40ft lugger *Happy Return* and had her rebuilt at Crowlas in 2003. Kitto had built her at Porthleven in 1905, for James Saunders of Folkestone. Saunders had lost his double-ended lugger *Good Intent* during a dramatic gale, and since it was under insured, the Mayor of Folkestone organized a public subscription to buy a new boat for him. In 1907 the *Happy Return* was fitted with a 7hp petrol-paraffin Kelvin engine. By 1998, under the name *Britannia* LN 224, she had probably become the oldest British boat still fishing. However her owner Pete Barrett, who had operated her from Swanage Bay for twenty-seven years, wanted to decommission her from fishing. Under the British Government's interpretation of EEC regulations she had to be cut up. This former lugger was at Cobbs Quay, Poole waiting to be sawn up the next day when, after a great deal of fighting the regulations, Pete Barrett managed to get an eleventh hour reprieve. So long as she was never used for commercial fishing again, it was agreed the Mount's Bay Lugger Association could restore her.

Porthleven

The first attempt to create a harbour at Porthleven was in 1818, but being on the exposed south-west coast it always had problems with swell breaking in. The first harbour was badly damaged by a gale and it was not until 1853, when Harvey & Co of Hayle bought the harbour, that it was more successful. They wanted to develop Porthleven as an outlet for the mining, but in spite of building two new piers the harbour never quite lived up to the grand plan. It did however become a considerable fishing centre during the nineteenth century boom in drift-netting. Because of the heavy swell breaking into harbour Porthleven, like Mousehole, is closed in the winter by putting baulks across the entrance and the boats fish from Newlyn.

Portmellon

Although it was far easier to work out of the harbour at Mevagissey, there appear to have been a few small boats crabbing out of the tiny cove just down the coast at Portmellon. The cottages at Portmellon have shutters to prevent salt water from being driven into them. This little hamlet made its name on the nautical map when Percy Mitchell opened a boatyard here in 1924. Born in 1901, Percy Mitchell was trained as a boat builder at Roberts in Mevagissey and when he went to Portmellon there was no yard there. Nor were there any facilities for launching craft, so he built a slipway in the cove and new boats had to be taken along the road to be launched. Mitchell's produced a stream of good quality wooden yachts and motor fishing vessels. The launch of the 72ft (21.95m) *Torbay Belle* was a major event and hundreds of people turned out to watch this. As she was too large to go down the road to the slipway she had to be launched over the sea wall. The 18ft open wooden *Mayblossom*, built in 1930, was one of the many toshers built by Mitchell. In 2001 this tosher was restored by George Dart, as the *Percy Mitchell*.

The Inner Harbour at Mevagissey in about 1930 with the ketch *Henrietta* being discharged. In the foreground are some 'Meva toshers', the open inshore fishing boats.

Mevagissey

It was pilchard fishing that led to the first stone pier being built at Mevagissey in 1470 and the Inner Harbour was started in about 1774. The easterly gales still roared right into the harbour until 1890, when the Outer Harbour wall was completed. There were numerous seine net companies operating from Mevagissey, but in the late nineteenth century decked driving luggers and smaller toshers were becoming more popular. There were eighty boats, which employed three hundred men, fishing from here when the Outer Harbour pier was built.

In the Victorian period East Cornish luggers shipped five hands when they went after mackerel in the winter. When they went for pilchard and herring in the summer they often had only three hands. In the summer the 'Meva' luggers used to go down to Newlyn and join boats from there, Looe, Polperro, Porthleven, Mousehole and St Ives for the 'pilchard drive' around Wolf Rock. When the whole fleet was there nets were being shot into the sea from about three hundred boats.

The Mevagissey toshers were open luggers and apparently, to avoid paying harbour dues, were kept under 20ft long. They were good sea boats with long fine bows and were used to fish for mackerel and hake and also to spin for whiting. Generally speaking, the sailing luggers from Mevagissey and Looe had transom sterns, but when motors came in the transom became general all over Cornwall.

The motorized lugger *Little Kate* at Mevagissey.

The first boat-building workshop was built in 1745 at the eastern corner of the harbour, which is now the museum. At the end of the Victorian era William Frasier was building luggers here, including, in 1904, the *Ibis* for Lakeman. In 1912 a 7hp Kelvin was put into the *Ibis* and in 1930 the Lakeman brothers had the larger 42ft *Ibis* built by Percy Mitchell. Originally this craft had two 7hp engines which gave her six knots, also a suit of sails helped get her home faster when there was a fair wind. In 1986 John Moore restarted wooden boat building in the eastern corner and launched a 34ft crabber for Newquay. In the 1980s John Moore & Son built open toshers and the 34ft *Britannia* for a Mevagissey owner. In 2002 Moore's were building a wooden boat for owners on the West Coast of Scotland.

Polperro

The first time I visited Polperro I was struck by its beauty and wondered why I had never been there before. The lady in one of the shops said, rather wearily 'I thought the whole world had been to Polperro.' Indeed in the summer it seems as if the whole world is trying to visit this truly beautiful village of white stone houses clinging to the side of a deep valley twisting back from the sea. The houses are packed tightly around the cove, which is sheltered, except when the wind is in the southeast.

A seine netting company for pilchards was not formed at Polperro until 1782. A man came from Mevagissey to show them how to work it and, although he fell out with the Polperro Company, the fishery was highly successful. Between 1888 and 1926 the building, that now houses the Polperro Maritime Museum, was a pilchard-packing factory owned by Teglios of Genova, an Italian family who also owned cellars at Looe. The salted pilchards in barrels were taken from here down to Fowey and loaded into schooners, and later steamers, and sent to Genova where they were eaten raw and considered a great delicacy. In 1912 over a million pilchards were landed in one day and fifty women worked ashore packing them into barrels. After World War I the Italian Government place a high tax on imported fish and this trade ended.

Although it was a successful fishing village in the medieval period the unprotected cove was a real problem in bad weather. In 1817 a severe gale smashed up thirty of the forty-five Polperro boats. The inner pier gave some protection, but in a gale the seas sent spray right over the Peak, a rock at the entrance. Another gale in the 1880s smashed up the Polperro clinker luggers and in 1891 a severe winter gale again destroyed many of the local boats. The only way that the boats could be saved in a southeast gale was to haul them up into the streets. The luggers were too big to move, so they were the ones that were smashed up.

Polperro in about 1900 with two barges and the fishing fleet of Polperro 'gaffers'. The hand operated storm barrier crane is in the foreground, on the harbour wall.

In the Victorian period there had been about forty boats working out of Polperro for the summer fishing. During bad weather in the winter the boats sometimes couldn't go out for six to eight weeks. On the sailing days the fishermen met on the quay around 6am and sometimes Tom Mark, one of the fishermen, would suddenly start preaching to the men as they stood there. In calm weather, when the whole fleet was at sea, drifting on the tide, the men in all the boats sometimes sang hymns.

The Polperro men had worked some luggers, but they preferred their smaller open sprit-sail-rigged 'spreeties', that were easier to row in and out of the cove. After the 1891 gale, when so many boats were destroyed that the village was destitute, a new type of boat involved for Polperro. When the first new gaffer arrived, a group of highly critical fishermen stood on the Peak, and expected the new boat to 'miss stays' when tacking in. In fact the new gaffer tacked successfully into the cove and soon most of the fishermen were ordering this new type, mostly from the builders Angear, Pearce and Ferris at Looe. The Polperro gaffers were totally different from all the other Cornish boats. They had outside ballast and a short pole mast setting a loose or 'soft' footed gaff sail. Both the 'spreeties' and gaffers were small enough to be rowed out of harbour until they could get clear of cliffs and pick up the wind.

To end the repeated damage to boats a storm barrier of baulks, planks lowered down into slots, was placed across the harbour mouth. Eight men were needed to operate the hand crane and two more on each end of the baulks to get them into place. Closing the harbour could take two hours, but in 1978 a gate, closed by electricity, was fitted.

The Polperro 'gaffers' in the harbour in about 1930.

When motors came in, the Polperro boats kept their sails. The lugger *Billy Bray*, which worked 7 miles of longline, kept her forelug and this was set on passage to the fishing grounds. Many sailing Cornish fishing boats were converted to yachts in the 1930s. Peter and Ann Pye's cutter *Moonraker* that was built in 1896 by Peter Ferris at Looe, started off as the 29ft Polperro gaffer *Lily*, and was sold in 1934 to the Pyes' who converted her to the yacht *Moonraker.* After World War II Dr Pye decided he didn't want to work in the new National Heath Service so they decided to live aboard *Moonraker,* and make a living writing and lecturing about their cruises. Through Peter Pye's books, *Moonraker* became one of the best-known cruising yachts of the period and inspired a whole generation of cruising yachtsmen.

The Polperro fleet declined and by 1953 there were five crabbing boats and about nine boats used for pilchards in season and long-lining in the spring, but the introduction of a fish market meant that in 2003 there were four trawlers and about eight small netters landing here.

Looe

Looe has a very sheltered harbour over-looked by the twin towns of East and West Looe, sitting on either side of a steep valley. Looe Island breaks the swell when the wind is in the southwest and the Banjo Pier, built in 1896, breaks the force of the seas in most other directions. When the wind is in the north the cliffs and high ground of Bodmin Moor break the force of the wind and the boats can work inshore in sheltered waters. There can be problems when the wind is in the east and the water is driven into the harbour and briefly into the Fore Street of East Looe.

East Looe was a major trading harbour with minerals, from the mines on Bodmin Moor, being brought down a canal to the riverside wharfs. Even after the canal closed, schooners still discharged at Buller's Quay, just inside the entrance. Behind this quay was the fishermen's quarter, seven narrow streets, known as the Back Streets, built on sand, which was taken from the middle of the harbour when the quay was built.

Peter and Ann Pye's Looe-built 29ft cutter *Moonraker* sai
British Columbia.

54

A small lugger at the quay at West Looe in 1889. The women in the foreground are salting pilchards into dome jars for use in the winter.

Seine netting for pilchards declined at Looe in the 1870s, but some pilchards were taken in the bay by a 40ft seine boat until the 1920s. Until about 1870 the pilchard boats of Looe, like the ones at neighbouring Polperro, were spritsail rigged. Later on a local transom version of the 40ft Cornish lugger was built at Looe. The smaller 22-28ft half-decked luggers, with a working area closed over by hatch boards, were worked inshore and known as 'quatters.' The men in the bigger luggers nicknamed these boats 'two men in a plank.' By the 1890s there was a fleet of forty decked luggers in Looe, as well as the small gaffers, and even some of the old spritsail boats were still working.

When it was a flat calm men were paid sixpence a time to haul the luggers out of the river. A block was placed on the end of the Banjo Pier and a rope was passed through it and out to the lugger. The men then ran back along the Banjo Pier hauling on the rope, so that the lugger was propelled out of the harbour. On the morning and afternoon neap tides the luggers anchored in the bay and 'scruffers'(boatmen) ferried the men and catch ashore. In a fog, known as 'ougee-mugee', a man stood on the Banjo Pier and 'called the luggers in' by shouting and later by blowing a whistle.

With forty luggers and eighteen schooners owned in Looe there was plenty of work for shipwrights. In the Victorian period the boat builders worked on any available space on the quays. Tom Pearce built luggers on the space in front of the present fishermen's stores. Later his son, Dick, built luggers at West Looe, just above the bridge. In 1997 a retired fisherman told me how in 1926 his mother had taken him down to the bridge to join the crowd watching the 38ft 'transom lugger' *White Heather*, when she was launched from

Luggers anchored off Looe in about 1912.

Pearce's yard. She had been built for the Thomas' at Mevagissey as there was no boat building there at that time. Dick Pearce's son 'Young Dick' also worked here and came out of retirement in World War II to help out at Curtis & Pape. His fine Victorian hand tools were much admired by his fellow shipwrights.

The Ferris', an off-shoot of the same family who built at Pill and Restronguet, moved up to be boat builders at Looe. Peter Ferris seems to have been the first to build luggers above the bridge, but before this, trading smacks and small ketches had been built on the Looe rivers. Getting new hulls down to West Looe quay for fitting was a tricky job. An anchor was sunk in the middle of the river below the bridge and at half tide the new hull was hauled through an arch on a block and tackle.

Harry Pearn, when he came out of the Royal Navy after World War I, started building in a shed above the Mill Pond, but in 1936 his sons Norman and Gerald, opened a building yard below the Mill Pond. Later Gerald moved to building in a workshop inland. Curtis and Pape had a yard up the West Looe River, well out of sight of the harbour. This yard closed in 1995 and no trace of it remains. The yard built yachts and, during World War II, large wooden MFVs.

After World War II drift netting for pilchard remained an important fishery at Looe. Until the 1950s the 'Salt Pits' on Buller's Quay, with the packing rooms above, were still sending salted pilchards to Italy in the traditional way, but most of the boats supplied Frank Curtis' canning factory. In the late 1950s cheaper canned pilchards came in from South Africa, and in spite of great protests in the town, the Curtis factory was forced to close. At least six factories in Cornwall were forced to close, which was a serious blow to the local fishing industry. There had been herring fishing at Looe, but in the 1930s the motor trawlers followed the herring into the sandy bays, where the fish were spawned, and kept fishing until the herring were all but gone. The Looe boats just worked from Plymouth or Brixham, but this was regarded as a very poor fishery. In 1965 the *Iris* and *Our Boys*, two motorized sailing luggers, were the last to go to Brixham for herring.

By 1960 there were only five decked boats fishing out of Looe. These were the *Our Boys*, *Our Girls*, *Eileen*, *Our Daddy* and the *Iris*. These boats were kept going by five men working them pilchard drifting at night and in the day two men took out shark-fishing parties. In 1971 the CFL (Cornwall Fishermen Ltd) was formed and this co-op opened a fish market at Looe in 1992 and the fishing fleet started to revive. The inshore mackerel fishery has returned and one day in the autumn of 2001, 24 tons of mackerel, all caught on Cornish 'jigging' hand-lines, were landed at Looe. In 2002 there were twenty-five trawlers and about fifteen inshore 'netters' landing at Looe and fish was also brought to the fish market 'overland' from other landings. Fish is sold to buyers from all over Western Europe.

One of the last of the motorized sailing luggers fishing from Looe was the 40ft *Guide Me*. She was built, with a 7hp Kelvin engine, at West Looe in 1911 by Peter Ferris, for W. Pengelly. As a new lugger, the *Guide Me* won the Kelvin Cup at the last of the original Looe Lugger Regattas that were sailed between 1897-1911. Although built for drift net fishing, the *Guide Me* also worked long-lines for conger, ray, turbot and ling. After over half a century of fishing under sail and power, the *Guide Me* was in bad order. When her skipper-owner Ned 'Pye' Pengelly died, the next owner didn't feel that it was worth investing in a rebuild for such an old boat, so the *Guide Me* was sold to owners in the Solent in the 1960s. A decade later she was a rotting hull lying in Fareham Creek. Here Jon and Judy Brickhill, attracted by her shapely hull, bought her and rebuilt and rigged her out again as a proper Cornish dipping lugger. The Brickhills cruised the *Guide Me*, without an engine, across the North Atlantic and then returned to live on her at Gweek. At the Looe Lugger Regattas the *Guide Me* has became the lugger that everyone struggles to beat.

When George Dart restored the *Our Boys* he rigged a standing lug foresail that saved the work of dipping the sail when tacking, but she always has to have a jib set. This powerful lugger was built by Dick Pearce at Looe in 1904 for George Woodrow Pengelly and fished from Looe for seventy-four years. In 1918 the Pengellys had the *Our Girls* built and launched with an engine. The *Our Girls* was fishing out of Looe until 1961. Then her 'engine driver' collapsed and later died at home. However the *Our Girls'* skipper said he used to see the 'engine driver' standing at his usual place when they returned from the fishing grounds and he refused to go to sea in her again. After that the Pengellys sold her.

The Looe boat *Emma Louise* and lugger *Guide Me* sailing into Looe, 1999.

Instead of walking from East Looe to West Looe over the bridge, it is quicker, when the tide is up, to take the short ride on one of the ferryboats. To operate in the shallow water the Looe ferryboats are almost flat bottomed. At sea these flat-bottomed clinker motorboats tend to pound, but they can creep into the harbour on a rising tide. These boats were built by Clifford Adams in his workshop in the Back Streets of East Looe and then manoeuvred through the narrow alleys and launched into the Looe River. The last Looe boat built was David Haines' *Emma Louise* in 1992 and part of the wall had to come down to get her out. After this Clifford Adam built several Redwings for the Looe Sailing Club. The *Emma Louise* is one of ten open boats, known as 'scruffers' in Looe, which put people off to boats anchor off the beach, undertake 'tripping' for visitors or take their turn at working the ferry across the river.

The gaffer Lady *Beatrice* at Polperro.

Chapter Three

SCHOONER PORTS

Coastal Ports in the Days of Sail

He who lives the longest sees the most
Austin Toms, The Looe pilot between 1930-39.

Monarchs of the Sea

The great sailing ships that returned home from their long ocean voyages were only on the horizon of the story of small sailing craft that worked around the coast, but two of the most famous square-riggers figured prominently in the history of the West Country.

The Finnish four-masted barque *Herzogin Cecilie* was wrecked on the Hamstone rocks near Bolt Head in 1936.

The Finnish four-masted barque *Herzogin Cecilie* had arrived at Falmouth in 1936 from Australia with wheat and sailed on for Ipswich. On her passage up the English Channel she failed to clear Bolt Head, near Salcombe and ran ashore on the Hamstone rocks. Much of her cargo was saved and most of the spars were removed and taken back to Finland, but she was never refloated.

The full-rigged ship *Cutty Sark* and the frigate *Foudroyant* at Falmouth in about 1935.

The famous tea clipper *Cutty Sark* had ended her trading days as a Portuguese brigantine, but in 1922 Captain W.H. Dowman, who had once been passed at sea by *Cutty Sark*, bought her and had her completely rigged out again. She became a nautical school, moored in Falmouth Harbour and boatmen used to run trippers out to her. Nearby was the *Foudroyant*, built as the Royal Navy frigate *Trincomalee* in 1817, which had been restored by Wheatley Cobb and also used as a training ship. In 1938 the *Cutty Sark* was towed to the Thames and *Foudroyant* went to Portsmouth.

Western Ocean Yachts
In the mid-nineteenth century the ship owners of the South Devon ports specialized in the Azores fruit trade. Their fast schooners raced back from St Michael's in the Azores with fresh oranges for the London market. After this they had to fight their way back against the prevailing winds in ballast. When steamers took over the Azores trade the deep draught fruit schooners dropped back into the far older Newfoundland salted cod trade. Salted cod, known as 'stockfish', was loaded in Newfoundland and taken across the Western Ocean to the Latin countries. The salted cod, like pilchards, was a cheap form of protein. The

schooners were often very well fitted out and became known as Western Ocean Yachts amongst seamen. The very last British schooner in the Newfoundland trade was the Kingsbridge-built *Lady St Johns* which made her last voyage in 1930. In 1928 she had made three eastward passages in an average of eighteen-and-a-half days.

The 112ft barquentine *Waterwitch* was the last British square-rigger trading. She was built in 1872 as a brig but to save manpower was 'cut down' to a barquentine for the coasting trade. She became one of a little group of sailing vessels owned by Edward Stephens, taking china clay north from Par and returning with coal. In 1935 Edward Stephens died and his small fleet was laid up and sold. After this a few British vessels, notably the three-masted tops'l schooner *Mary Miller* and the two-masted tops'l schooner *Katie,* carried cargoes under sail until the start of World War II. This was the end of an era.

The three-masted topsail schooner *Rhoda Mary* entering Newlyn with 179 tons of coal in 1924. This was the last freight she carried. The *Rhoda Mary,* built by Ferris, at Penpol Pill in 1868, was a very narrow schooner, noted for her speed.

The barquentine *Waterwitch*, the last British trading square rigger, laid up at Par in 1937.

Captain Greet's schooner *Rothersand*, a German-built steel vessel seized as a war prize after World War I, sheltering in St Ives during a north-west gale in April 1930.

The lugger *Our Boys* at the start of the 1995 Looe Lugger Regatta.

The lugger *Our Boys* passing a Looe scalloper, 2002.

Paul Greenwood fitting out his *Our Boys* at Looe, 2003

The lugger *Reliance* being rowed out of Looe on the ebb tide.

The Home Trade

In the mid-Victorian period every port was alive with small sailing ships. Places that are quiet backwaters today were major shipping centres with shipowners, shipbuilders and their own seafaring community. Not many new coastal sailing ships were built after about 1905, because there was a steady decline in trade. Many small ports started to die out because steamers and the railways centralized goods distribution, but then came World War I, 'The War to end all Wars,' which created a boom in freight rates and small ships and small ports went through a brief boom period.

A few new sailing vessels were actually built just after the Great War, but in 1921 the boom ended and freight rates collapsed. At the same time road transport began to rob the small coastal vessels of their short-haul freights. Hundreds of small ports turned to yachting and tourism to replace schooners and ketches.

Newquay is typical of the small 'lost ports'. The earliest port here was just up the coast in the River Gannell, but this dried out at low tide. In the fifteenth century a 'Newquay' was built on the coast to save the difficulties of getting into the Gannell. In 1833 Robert Lomax built a harbour enclosing four acres at Newquay. The main trade was shipping out minerals from the mines and china clay.

In the Victorian period around one hundred and fifty vessels were owned here, but the port declined rapidly and the last outward-bound freight went

The ketch *Electric* 'making sail' as she leaves Watchet. The men in the boat are hobblers, unofficial pilots who helped the vessels out of the harbour by hauling them along the harbour wall or by towing them out with a pulling boat.

in 1921 in the Appledore ketch *Hobah*. The steel ketch *Hanna* took the last freight in, the following year. The loss of faith in sea borne trade was reflected in the local council's plan to dam up the Gannell. An enterprising man bought the topsail schooner *Ada* and kept her in the Gannell so that he could claim that it was still used by sea-going ships.

Every task on the sailing ships was done by hand labour. The freight was carried ashore on the men's backs in two and a quarter cwt (2377kgs) bags. At Gloucester and Sharpness it was said that a 'boy' became a 'man' when he could carry a two and a quarter cwt bag on his back and 'lump'(throw) it under the decks.

A trading ketch and topsail schooner at Newquay about 1909.

The ketch *Orestes* sailing from Minehead on the evening tide in the summer of 1924.

The steel 3-masted topsail schooner *S.F.Pearce* discharging cement by hand at Falmouth.

While the sea was the only way to move bulk goods the little ports were active. There was regular trade into Boscastle and some schooners were built there. Bude had a fleet of about twenty schooners and ketches owned in the town. Some Bude vessels were built on the Strand before the canal, but most of the schooners were built at Stapleton's yard on the Canal Upper Basin. Bude men like Orlando 'Flanders' Jewel went to sea because there was little employment in the coastal towns. Besides, by going to sea these men had a chance of getting a better income. Orlando became master of the topsail schooner *Lord Devon*, trading to Flanders, and although he had fallen from the mast and permanently injured his leg, he still went in sail and ended up as skipper of the Tamar barge *Kate*.

The ketch *St Agnes* discharging on the Percuil River.

Orlando 'Flanders' Jewell at his home in King Street, Bude in 1962, looking at Reuben Chappell's ship portrait of the topsail schooner *Lord Devon* which he had been captain of between 1914-20.

There was around 20ft of water over the bar at Bude at high water but the groundswell made it one of the most difficult places to get a schooner in. Even in calm weather there were occasions when the swell suddenly rolled in from the Atlantic. A westerly or northerly blow would also pile seas up on the bar. It was bad enough for a laden vessel to enter, but when beating out, light, it was even more dangerous because if the vessel 'missed stays' (failed to turn round) it simply ploughed ashore. In spite of the difficulties, about three vessels a week entered Bude. Many local vessels were lost here, particularly in the winter. Once the railway arrived in 1898 the trade to the harbour slowly died. Most owners did not replace their vessels, as they were wrecked or worn out.

When Walter Petherick was over ninety, he was very keen to keep his ketch *Ceres* going. In 1936 this 125 year-old vessel was finally lost outside the Appledore bar. After this only the steel motor ketch *Traly* traded to Bude. On small neap tides the *Traly* had to stop in the channel and discharge part of her cargo before she could get into the lock. The *Traly* delivered the last freight, into Bude, in 1946.

The Bristol Channel pilot cutter *Veteran* with the steel ketch *Traly* discharging in the Bude Canal in 1941. The *Veteran* was Dr Grindley's yacht that had been brought around from Falmouth to be clear of the bombing.

Captain Ken Shaw's motor barge *Eldorita* entering Portreath, 1962.

The coaster *Fredanja* of Haren entering Portreath in 1939. The coaster was eventually lost off Copelands in 1940.

Wherever there was freight to be moved someone built a harbour, although some did not survive after the schooner era. A harbour was created at St Agnes in 1632 but the sea kept washing it away. Because an outlet was needed for the local mines, a fourth harbour was built, and in the Victorian period schooners were built and owned here. When the trade died, the harbour was not maintained, and the last one was washed away in the 1920s.

The tiny fishing cove at Portreath was developed from about 1770 as a harbour to bring in Welsh coal and the inner basin was built in 1846 as an outlet for the mines in Gwennap. In 1880 D.W. Bain & Co operated sixteen ketches and schooners from Portreath. The Atlantic groundswell made entering the harbour a nightmare, even in calm weather. This was bad enough in powered vessels, but the schooners had to be warped in.

Pentawan, on the south-east Cornish coast, was constructed between 1818-26 so that minerals and china clay could be shipped out. Almost at once it started to silt up and in 1870 reservoirs were created to build up water to scour the harbour out. The last freight of china clay was shipped out in 1929 and the last ship locked out in 1940, after which the harbour was closed by silt.

The silted up harbour at Pentewan, 1981.

The ketch *Humility* of Bideford and barquentine *Donna Louisa* in Appledore Pool.

Appledore

The Rivers Torridge and Taw cut deep valleys into the green hills of North Devon and where they meet sits the little town of Appledore. The shipbuilding yard remains busy, but the narrows streets of Appledore lead down to an empty, windswept quay. The main reminder of the town's maritime past is in the North Devon Maritime Museum on Odun Road.

When the steamers drove the small sailing ships out of the deep water trades, and many of the home trades, the ports of South Devon looked to yachting and tourism, while Cornwall still had fishing and in the summer every train brought another party of tourists. There was tourism to North Devon, but very little around Bideford and Appledore. Men still looked to the sea for a living, because there was little alternative.

Two three-masted schooners motoring around Land's End in about 1930. Because they were fitted with low-powered engines the square sail on the foremast had been removed to cut down on the number of hands needed.

In the nineteenth century the sailing ships of Appledore traded to Canada, while the 'Down Homers' stayed on the coast. The term 'down home' originally meant returning from the Bristol Channel and crossing the Bideford bar. To continue west was to go 'down and along' and then 'round the Land' into the 'Channel.'

During the inter-war trade slump, and because of considerable competition from Dutch coasters, built with Government subsidies, most sailing ship owners were forced to sell their vessels. The North Devon owners actually saw it as a chance to acquire fresh vessels cheaply. The men of Appledore, Bideford, Barnstaple and Braunton, all inside Bideford bar, begun buying up vessels at knock down prices. Their secret was that they fitted engines at once, and even a low-powered one meant that freights could be delivered much quicker.

Appledore remained a true sailing ship port, with all the skills such as sailmakers and shipwrights needed to keep small wooden vessels at sea until after World War II. There was usually a little forest of masts off Appledore Quay, made up of vessels home from trading, while little groups of men hung around exchanging gossip about their friends and neighbours who were scurrying about the Bristol Channel in these motor-sail vessels.

The schooners and ketches were run on something of a shoestring, but with freight rates so low in the inter-war years the economics were even tighter. When the 62ft ketch *AT* arrived at Bude in 1937 with 80 tons of basic slag the crew had to unreeve the mainsheet to moor her up in the lock because they did not have any other strong ropes. The *AT*, which by then had a 30hp Widdop Invincible hot bulb engine, was put up for sale at £70, but anyone who bought her could only expect to 'buy a job' as the ketch would only have earned a wage and little return on the investment.

The 94ft ketch *Two Sisters* got her 30hp Widdop Invincible engine second-hand out of the brigantine *Maggie G* of Poole, which was wrecked in 1928 at Marsland Mouth. As this was on the county boundary it caused some administrative problems for Lloyds as some of the wreckage was in Devon and some in Cornwall. Eventually the engine found its way to Appledore shipyard and into the *Two Sisters*.

The smaller North Devon vessels were 'Down Homers', just trading around Bristol Channel while the larger vessels went anywhere, but by the 1930s they had only a few trades left. They moved coal and grain from the ports in South Wales down to the small ports in the West Country, while the larger vessels carried coal across to Southern Ireland and took some china clay freights.

The Appledore three-masted schooner *Kathleen & May* at Plymouth during the time the Maritime Trust were attempting to preserve her in 1976.

One of the Appledore schooners was the *Kathleen & May*, built as a three-masted topsail schooner in North Wales in 1900. M.J. Fleming of Youghal had owned her and in 1931 she became one of the 'bargains' snapped up by the North Devon owners. Her skipper owner Tommy Jewell personified the true Appledore seafarer. He spent his whole career at sea in vessels owned by his family, apart from just six months. Tommy Jewell kept the *Kathleen & May* in very good order and when he was not at sea, he returned to his home in the little narrow streets just back from Appledore Quay.

During World War II *Kathleen & May* was running with coal across to Southern Ireland, often with an Irish crew. Tommy Jewell also brought sacks of potatoes back to a hungry Britain, these were kept in a little store in an Appledore back street and were sold to his neighbours. Once, in August 1940 when the *Kathleen & May* was anchored off Barry, the ketch *Irene* came in and her captain asked to borrow a man to get back to Lydney. The *Irene* had finished discharging coal at Courtmacsherry when the Irish crew left because they would not risk a wartime crossing. Sixty-eight year-old Captain Andrew Murdock then sailed back to Barry single-handed, getting very little rest during the passage that took four days and three nights.

The schooner *Ryelands* was issued with a Lewis gun to defend herself during the War, but her skipper Ken Shaw tried a different approach. While on passage to Ireland a German Heinkel fighter circled around, trying to work out what they were. One of the Irish crew ran for the Lewis gun, but Ken told him to leave that alone and hang a neutral Irish flag over the rail. He then told the crew to lean on the rail casually and give the German fighter a friendly wave next time it went over. The trick worked, but after that *Ryelands* tried to stay in the Bristol Channel and down the south west coast.

The Bideford and Bristol Shipping's 85ft *Devonia* at Bude in about 1935. This steamer was built in 1894 to run a packet service between Bideford and Bristol.

Peter Herbert of Bude went to sea in the Appledore vessels just after World War II. There was still an active fleet of motor sailers enjoying the post-war demand for coastal tonnage but everybody knew that the days of the small sailing vessels were over. Peter asked if he could buy the 80ft ketch *Progress*, which had been in the Newfoundland trade, loaded 150 ton and with a 36hp Ellwe engine. Old Fred Harris said 'I don't want to take this young man's £1,750, knowing that he can't succeed.'

The trading ketch *Bessie Clark* at Bude in about 1938. Walter Petherick and Captain Bob Tucker are on the hatch and Treby Barrett and Jack Lewis on the rail.

The *Progress* was sold to become a yacht, while Peter bought the little ketch *Agnes*, in 1954. She only loaded 107 tons, but he managed to keep her in trade for two years. Due to his enthusiasm for keeping the vessels in trade he reopened several ports, for a few more

Peter Herbert's ketch *Agnes* after her head rope broke and she swung across the river at Wadebridge in 1955.

years. The last vessel at Wadebridge on the River Camel had been the Appledore ketch *Bessie* in 1943. After this owners of motor schooners and ketches refused to send their vessels there until Peter Herbert agreed to take a freight up to Wadebridge twelve years later in the *Agnes*. The Padstow pilot Tommy Morrissey took the ketch up to Wadebridge Mill. However in mooring up Peter under-estimated the force of the ebb tide under the bridge, and the ketch's head ropes parted, which forced her to swing across the channel. An old man, who had been leaning on the bridge watching, came over and said 'I've been waiting for that to happen. To hold her you should have a rope running to the top window of the mill.'

Loading the ketch *Agnes* at Barry for a Cornish port, 1955.

After the *Agnes*, several other vessels went up to Wadebridge. Peter never delivered freights under sail, he always had to keep the engine running. All these North Devon vessels were true auxiliaries, using sail and low-powered engines. Once a huge hole had been cut in a rudder for the propeller the vessel lost her grip on the water and would not sail properly.

The ketch *Agnes* passing Trevose Head 'bound down the land.' 1955.

The Appledore auxiliary vessels held these trades because it was uneconomic to haul goods all the way round from South Wales to the West Country by land. After World War II larger lorries were introduced and Britain slowly improved her road system. By the 1960s the writing was on the wall for the end of the small coasters, as well as the few ancient motor-sailers that were still plodding their way around to the coastal ports. In order to compete against road transport, coastal ships became larger but were then unable to enter many of the smaller ports.

One by one the North Devon vessels gave up. In 1960 the schooner *Kathleen & May* and the ketch *Irene* were laid up at Appledore Quay for sale. The *Result* was still going, but then she was really a motor ship. The tragedy of these vessels is that although they lasted until after World War II, it was not quite long enough for the big revival of interest in traditional craft.

Peter Herbert's Bude ketch *Agnes* at Hayle in May 1955 laden with best Welsh Powells Tilleries steam coal, from Cardiff, destined for Tehidy Hospital.

The St Ives pilot Dan Paynter in his ex-lugger coming alongside the motor ship *Gardience* in 1950. The *Gardience* was on a regular contract running coal from Barry to the power station at Hayle.

Some were sold to become yachts. The *Agnes* was wrecked in the West Indies, the 63ft *Isabel*, another little trading ketch, was wrecked in South America. Those that have survived have only done so by luck. *Kathleen & May* became a museum ship on the Thames and was happily rotting away until she was taken, with pumps running, on a heroic tow around Land's End to Gloucester Dock. From here Steve Clarke took her back to Bideford, rebuilt her and trips were made back to her old trading grounds in Southern Ireland where she received an overwhelming welcome.

The ketch *Irene*, after a few false starts, fell into the hands of Leslie Morrish who spent decades getting her back into good sailing order. For a time she was based on the River Tamar, but was then sailed to the West Indies. The ketch *Garlandstone* is a museum ship up the River Tamar. The 77ft ketch *Bessie Ellen*, which loaded 148 tons, was built by William Kelly at Mountbatten, Plymouth in 1907 and sold new to an owner at Braunton. In 1947 she was sold to Danish owners and spent the next fifty-three years there, including being rebuilt at Troense. Nikki Alford, who had been first mate on Square Sail's barque *Kaskelot,* bought her at Ring Andersens famous yard at Svendborg and brought her back to Plymouth to do charter work. The *Bessie Ellen* was then rigged out and given a 310hp Volvo Penta engine, a far cry from her first engine, the 25hp Widdop that had been fitted in 1916. How the old-timers would have loved to have a 310hp engine to punch them around the headlands against a foul tide.

Local Trades
In the Victorian era many ports had trading smacks, single-masted gaff cutters, in purely local trade. The small trading smacks and ketches landed cargoes in the summer on any reasonably sheltered beach. On the north Cornish coast cargoes were brought ashore at Tintagel, Trebarwith and many other sheltered beaches. Little traders brought in coal from South Wales to Trebarwith Strand and took out Delabole slate. The patch of sand, now popular with surfers, had the rather grand name of Port William, but because of the groundswell it must have been a bad place for putting a small wooden vessel ashore. However there had been trade in here for at least sixty years.

The Falmouth barge *The Sirdar* sailing in Carrick Roads with a new mainsail.

By the 1920s most of the small traders had gone, but small craft still worked, at Falmouth, Plymouth and Barnstaple. At Falmouth the larger 'outside' smacks were usually round-bottomed. One of the fastest of these was *The Sirdar*, which until the outbreak of World War II was carrying her 50ton cargoes along the south coast of Cornwall and Devon under sail with a crew of two men. After World II *The Sirdar* was sold to Portuguese owners and the last of these 'inside' flat-bottomed barges, the Helford River 'little' *Industry*, was converted to the yacht *Deerhound*. She finished up as a houseboat at Aldeburgh where she was burnt in 1985.

Captain Edwin Bryant's trading ketch *Diligent*, in the Inner Harbour, Mevagissey in about 1930.

The 23 tons net register ketch *W.E.Gladstone*.

The ketch *W. E.Gladstone* sailing in Falmouth Bay

The ketch *W.E.Gladstone* anchored at Fowey and the three-masted schooner believed to be the steel German-built war prize *S.F.Pearce*.

The Dutch tjalk *London Premier* discharging at Porthleven in about 1938.

Josiah Hunkin of Mevagissey had small vessels trading into Porthleven, Fowey and Polperro. He had the the 23 ton *W.E.Gladstone* which had been built as a lugger at St Ives, proved to be too large to be economic, and was converted to a trading ketch. The Hunkin family also had the *Shortest Day*, another large lugger converted to a cargo ketch. In 1930 the *W.E.Gladstone* got ashore in the Helford River and was lost. She was replaced by the Dutch steel tjalk *London Premier* which traded until about 1939.

There had been small barges taking goods from Padstow up the River Camel to Wadebridge. All around the coast there were dozens of small local trades involving craft unique to that area, but following World War I they vanished one by one. The last barges loaded gravel on Crow Point in front of Braunton Burrows where the Rivers Taw and

North Devon sailing gravel barges off Instow in about 1910.

The luggers *Reliance* and *Ibis* passing the Banjo Pier, East Looe.

Luggers *Ibis*, *Ocean Pride*, *Pet*, *Guiding Star*, *Guide Me* and *Our Boys* waiting for the afternoon race at the Looe Lugger Regatta, 2003.

The lugger *Guide Me* setting her mizzen topsail before passing *Marget* to start a race in the Looe Lugger Regatta, 2003.

The *Guide Me* dipping her forelug to pass the yard head forward of the mast when tacking.

The lugger *Reliance* under a press of sail.

The dandy *Guiding Star*, tosher *Percy Mitchell* and dandy *Our Daddy* off Looe.

Mike Darlington on the dandy *Our Daddy* in Plymouth Sound.

Polperro's restored 1902 Looe RNLI lifeboat *Ryder* and Newlyn lugger *Ocean Pride.*

Terry Grace's gravel barges *Marlene Grace* and *Louisa Grace* waiting to load gravel on Crow Point with Appledore in the background, 1984.

Torridge meet. This was loaded over the side at low water, taken up to Bideford and Barnstaple on the flood tide and sold to the local builders. The first of these barges to be built with an engine was the 49ft *Result* by Harris at Appledore in 1922 and the following year the *JJRP* by Philip Waters at Appledore. Within a decade there was not enough work for all the gravel barges and some were given away, sound and fully rigged, by their owners just to get rid of them. Others were fitted with engines and carried on, but the *Hilda* still had her sails until about 1948.

In 1970 three firms were paying the Crown Commissioners to load gravel on Crow Point. Terry Grace steadily bought up the barges so that he became the last operator taking gravel. By then barges were being loaded by tractors with a front-end loader and could work sixteen tides in every month up to Brunswick Wharf, Barnstaple. The last wooden barge in this work was the *Result* that was withdrawn in 1984 after which Terry Grace operated two steel barges. There was a great deal of friction with conservationist over this ancient trade. Terry Grace walked the coast down as far as Crackington Haven and found that the tide carried everything north. Stones on Crow Point came from around Buck's Mills. In 2000 the Planning Permission was withdrawn and Terry Grace's barges were laid up at Barnstaple.

Polruan

In 1789 William Geach was running a shipbuilding yard at Polruan. This yard went bankrupt in 1837 and after 1847 J. Slade & Sons were building wooden barquentines and schooners for the ocean trades. Slade's closed in 1943 and Daphne du Maurier, the novelist who lived at Menabilly, bought one yard and Norman Humkin ran it. One of Slades' blacksmiths, Charlie Toms, also started building yachts at Polruan. The Toms yard has expanded to take over most of the Polruan waterfront and is run by Charlie's grandson. By 2003 Alan Tom's yard, and one in Macduff, were the only yards left in Britain that regularly built wooden fishing boats.

The schooner *Esmeralda* and the steam ship *Albion* at Calstock. This port, 24 miles up the River Tamar, was once very busy with minerals and farm products being shipped out. The railway and viaduct opened in 1908 and within five years the river trade had finished. The foot ferry closed in 1969.

A Plymouth barge discharging stone on the beach at Leas Foot Sands, Thurleston, South Devon in about 1910.

The Falmouth 'outside barge' *The Sirdar* had her auxiliary engine running and her mainsail set ready to catch the breeze as she was leaving Polperro in about 1932.

Ketch discharging at Polperro in front of the pilchard factory.

Looe

Looe was the outlet for the mining district inland. Goods came down the canal and by rail. The railway track at East Looe went right down through the present Fish Market to Buller's Quay near the river mouth. Austin Toms recorded that when the 114ft barquentine *Florence* was launched off the sea front at East Looe in 1869 it was so shallow that they had difficulty getting her to float. On the other hand one of the schooners launched at West Looe, from just south of St Nicholas Church, charged across the river and her counter stern knocked a gas lamp bracket off a wall. To avoid harbour dues limestone was unloaded from barges on the beach in front of East Looe and horses and carts took it up through the narrow streets to the limekilns inland. There was also a brickworks at Hannafore, before the hotels were built, and barges loaded on the cliff foot there. After World War II the trade into Looe was handled by the Thames ship owners, Everards . This was mainly cement from the Thames, discharged at Buller's Quay and timber discharged further up near the bridge, from the Baltic. Once one of Everard's sailing barges brought a freight in a week late and held up the builders in the town. Freights shipped out were hay and dung to the Channels Islands. It seems that the last freight into Looe was in about 1957. Four years later the first fishermen's cottages were turned into self-catering holiday flats and the warehouses were also converted into shops and flats as Cornwall switched to tourism as its main industry.

A trading ketch with legs to keep her upright at Polperro in about 1930. Cargoes from the barges and schooners were taken inland through the narrow streets in horse drawn carts.

The Plymouth barge *P.H.E.* at Buller's Quay, East Looe in about 1930.

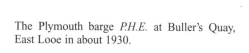

The Everard coaster *Fred Everard* discharging cement at Buller's Quay, East Looe in about 1950.

Charlestown Charter Ships

In the eighteenth century ships bringing goods to St Austell discharged on the open beach at West Polmear. The landowner Charles Rashleigh decided to have a harbour constructed in the cove in order to ship out copper from his mines. In 1801 Rashleigh commissioned John Smeaton, the builder of Eddystone Lighthouse, to build a harbour, that he named Charlestown. Later work at the tiny harbour concentrated on exporting china clay and the occasional coasting vessel was still coming in to load in 2001.

After the Rashleighs sold the Charlestown Estate, which included the harbour and houses, it changed hands frequently. In 1971 the lock was widened from 27ft to 35ft to let bigger ships in. In 1973 Martin and Sarah Pumphrey started the Cornish Smoked Fish Co and they smoke and retail fish at the top of Charlestown Harbour.

A three-masted topsail schooner and a steamer loading china clay at Charlestown in about 1920.

The brigantine *Marques* entering Charlestown, 1974.

In 1974 Robin Cecil Wright and Mark Litchfield bought the Spanish trading coasting schooner *Marques* and converted her to a brigantine. The *Marques* was rigged out at Charlestown and based here. Later the *Marques* was converted to a barque and used in the BBC series on Charles Darwin. In 1984 she was lost in a strong squall 80 miles off Bermuda.

Robin and Tony Davies started charter work on the East Coast from Brightlingsea in 1967 with the Baltic ketch *Clausens Minde*. By concentrating on filmwork the Davies brothers built up Square Sail, a fleet of wooden, mostly ex-Baltic, sailing ships. Square Sail were constantly searching for a good base for their ships. They used the West India Dock, London then Gloucester Dock and Bristol and eventually in 1994 moved to Charlestown, at which point Tony left for New Zealand with the brigantine *Soren Larsen*.

Robin Davies' Square Sail turned Charlestown into a sailing ship port. In the summer the ships sail away on film or promotional charters and return to Charlestown for their winter refit. The 120ft wooden barque *Kaskelot,* built in 1947 by Ring Andersen for the Danish Government as a motor schooner to take supplies along the coast of Greenland, lies near the lockgate. Others on the fleet include the barque *Earl of Pembroke*, another former wooden Baltic trader, and the 'pocket tall ship' *Phoenix*, now a brig, which was built in Denmark in 1929 as a trading schooner. These ships often change rigs and names for different films, although Square Sail tries to have a ship for each period of history.

The *Gwendoline* and three other Tamar barges loading on the lower quay at Calstock in about 1910.

Newman's brigantine *Harrier* being towed out of Dartmouth in about 1870.

Chapter Four

PILOT CUTTERS, SMACKS AND WORK BOATS.

Gaff-Rigged Workboats in the West Country

We pray thee Lord, not that shipwrecks should happen, but if any wrecks should happen,
that they be guided into the Scilly Isles.
Scillonian prayer

Scillonian Pilot Cutters

In the sailing ship era any vessels coming in from the Atlantic 'closing the land' at the end of a voyage had very little idea of their exact position. Many were wrecked either on the Isles of Scilly or running into the cliffs of Cornwall. Since, apart from smuggling and a little farming and trading, the Scillonians had very limited employment, men were glad to develop a pilot service.

The Scillonian pilots cruised at sea in pilot cutters or raced out from the land in pilot gigs. Highly seaworthy craft were needed to go out into the huge seas of the open Atlantic. Since the pilot cutters were in competition, they needed to be fast to reach the incoming ship first and put their pilot aboard.

The first Scillonian pilot cutter was built in 1793 and the last one in 1875. These pilot cutters varied in length from 35-60ft and had a small hatch aft of the mainmast so that cargoes could be carried between the islands. By the 1880s competition from the pilots working from Falmouth led to a decline in work for the Scillonian pilots, but the gigs went on until World War I. The last of the Scillonian pilot cutters was the 46ft *Agnes* built in 1841. She was sold in 1894 and after that, used to bring coal from South Wales to heat the greenhouses on Scilly, as daffodil growing had become the main economy of the islands. In 1902 the *Agnes* was broken up on Tresco and used for fencing posts.

By using the available information, a half model, dimensions, and photographs, Luke Powell built the new wooden Scillonian pilot cutters at Gweek. Starting with the 37ft *Eve of St Mawes* in 1997, the 42ft *Lizzie May* in 2001, the 42ft *Agnes* in 2003 and then started work on the 44ft *Hesper*.

Falmouth Quay Punts

The Falmouth quay punts sailed out into the Atlantic to get runners (salesman) aboard incoming ships. The runners returned with orders for chandlers, tailors and other tradesmen in the town and when the ships arrived in Falmouth the goods were delivered. In the summer the quay punts took part in races and took visitors sailing around the harbour.

These little yawls were called quay punts because they were based at the Customs House Quay. They had short masts so that they did not catch the spars of the sailing ships when they went alongside.

One surviving quay punt is the 28ft *Louis Will*, built by W.E. Thomes at Falmouth in 1900. She was working until 1938 when she became a yacht and was rebuilt by John Fuge

Alun Davies hauling an oyster dredge on his Falmouth work boat *Iris Elizabeth*, 1999.

The new Scillonion pilot cutter *St Anges* and dandy *Our Daddy*, 2003.

The barques *Kaskelot* and *Earl of Pembroke* and brig *Phoenix* at Charlestown, 2002

The former sailing trawler *Vigilance* at Brixham 2003. Upham yard, where she built, was just to the left, but has now been built over as holiday flats.

A Falmouth Quay punt racing in Falmouth Harbour about 1910.

A Falmouth quay punt carrying holiday makers on a trip in about 1936.

in 1990-95 for Charles Ford. Another surviving quay punt is the 26ft *Greenshank* that was built by R.S.Burt in 1914. Charles Burt had a shipyard at Ponsharden and built trading schooners while his son R.S.Burt built the quay punts. Charles' nephew E.J.Burt was also a boat builder at T.Jackett's former yard in the High Street. Motor quay punts replaced the sailing punts in the 1930s.

The Falmouth Quay punt *Louis Will* on her mooring in the Fowey River, 2002.

Falmouth Work Boats

Originally the oysters on the 'banks' of the River Fal were dredged by smacks from the South and East Coast and they were used to replenish young stock. The oyster stocks in the Fal and Helford River must have been considerable when it is considered that over a hundred smacks from the East Coast had arrived at times to take oysters. By 1840 there was considerable friction between the East Coast men and Cornishmen over dredging, as it had become apparent that oyster stocks needed to be controlled. However it was nearly twenty years before the oyster stocks became solely under local control.

The Truro Oyster and Mussel Fishery Order of 1876 is still in operation and does not permit oysters to be dredged during the winter season by any powered craft. As well as sail-boats working the 'banks' at the edge of the main channel of Carrick Roads, small open boats operate in shallow water. In Falmouth these boats were known as 'hal toe' (haul tow) punts while at Restronguet and further up the river they were 'dredging boats.' However it still required hard manual work to operate them. The method of operating is to drop the anchor, drift back on the tide, drop in a dredge and haul it back over the ground by winching it up to the anchor. Since in nautical terms a hand-operated winch is a 'wink' the punts were sometimes referred to as winks.

The Loe and Feock Regatta in 1909. The two pulling boats on the right are 'dredging boats'.

Haul and tow punts at Mylor Dockyard in 1969.

Haul and tow punts racing at Mylor as part of the November 5 Race, 1984.

Dredger men used to buy coastal luggers and convert them to gaff cutters, because dredging oysters was only allowed for about three months in the early winter, which did not always justify building a new boat. Many of these early luggers were of too deep draught for working on the banks at low water and it became more practical to built workboats with a 3ft 6ins draft, but they retained the straight stem and stern of the luggers.

The *Morning Star*, which was worked in the Truro River fishery until 1980, had an incredibly long career in the sea and oyster fishery in the Falmouth area.

The 30ft Falmouth workboat *George Glasson* 'drifting' sideways with the tide down over the oyster 'banks' in the Carrick Roads, 1974.

The 32ft *Morning Star* was already an old lugger, probably built in about 1840, when she was converted to a gaff cutter for oyster-dredging in about 1890. The gaff-rig allowed the craft to move sideways while she 'drifted' across the oyster banks towing dredges. Another former lugger is the *George Glasson*, built at Porthleven in 1898. She was known as a 'half boat' because she was decked forward of the mast. She was used as a pilchard driver, for long-lining and trawling. In 1923 she was bought by an oyster dredgerman and converted to a gaff cutter rig, a much more versatile rig for tacking 'back up' when dredging. The *Morning Star* was dredging until she was run down and sunk on her mooring at Restronguet in 1980.

The fortunes of the Truro River Oyster Fishery have waxed and waned. At times during the Victorian period there were fifty sail-boats working, but the highest number in the twentieth century was forty-five in 1922. The men who worked the boats called them Truro River oyster boats, but Falmouth workboats became the accepted term for them. After World War II most oystermen working in Carrick Roads thought this archaic sail-only fishery would fade out when the wooden boats were worn out. However the very hard winter of 1962-3 killed off stocks on the East Coast and oyster prices rose after this. This gave the younger men confidence to order new boats, mostly from Terry Heard. Terry, a dredgerman turned boat-builder, started a boatyard at Tregatreath on Mylor Creek and built four wooden-hulled workboats. The dredgermen, finding them too expensive, asked for a cheaper hull and Terry Heard decided to start a new class of GRP workboats.

Falmouth workboats racing in about 1968. Left to right *Sercia*, *Victory*, *Magdalena*, *St Meloris* and *Stella*.

Terry Tuffery left, on the Falmouth workboat *Softwings* sailing in Carrick Roads, 1981.

In 1969 there were thirty-five boats dredging and in 1972 Terry Heard built the first GRP 28ft workboat *Melorus*. She was used as a yacht, but in 1973 the *Three Sisters* became the first of this two-man workboat class to go oyster dredging. This class was designed by Percy Dalton and he also designed the one-man 22ft class of workboats, the first of which was the *Carrie* in 1978. The same year Heard's produced their first GRP punt, perhaps more significant was the building, that year, of 28ft *Rebecca* for 'Doc' Phil Slater, which was built to win workboat races. After this there were two separate classes of workboats. Dredgers worked in the winter and the racers, carrying a large sail plan and using yacht's hand winches, competed in the summer.

Although other boat-builders turned out the occasional workboat, Terry Heard's enthusiasm for these boats was a major part of their development. Sadly this immensely popular man died in 1985 when he was only fifty-seven. However his son, the charismatic Martin Heard, took on running the yard. In Martin's era the demand has been largely for pleasure craft.

Charles Harker's 24ft workboat *Shamrock*, leaving the Custom Quay, Falmouth in 1988.

Although the upsurge of interest in workboats has meant that many old boats have been rebuilt, it is unusual for them to keep to the traditional appearance of the pre-Heard period. However the 24ft *Shamrock*, built as a lugger at Mevagissey in 1908 and fished from Scilly before being converted to an oyster-dredger, was rebuilt and fitted out with traditional round spars.

The oyster disease Bonamia reached the Carrick Roads in 1981 and instead of over twenty boats, only a few dredged. In 1984-5 only six boats and some punts dredged oysters. In 1989-90, just *Katherina* and Mike Parson's *Leila* dredged full-time, with *Rhoda Mary*, *Three Sisters, Zona* and *Shamrock* doing some dredging.

The Truro River oyster fishery recovered from Bonamia and about twenty boats returned to dredging. The only other similar fishery was in Chesapeake Bay on the eastern seaboard of the United States, but the boats there were much larger and more expensive to operate. By 2000 only two sailboats were taking parties out dredging. This means that the Falmouth workboats are the only fleet of working sailing craft in the developed western world. The original wording of the by-law of this unique fishery was intended to keep steamboats out, but it has also proved a very successful form of conservation because the sailboats have never exhausted the stock of oysters.

Mike Parsons while oyster dredging on the *Leila*, 1969.

The steel yacht *Ultima Thule* ashore at Wherrytown, Mount's Bay in 1979. She was dragged off the beach by a tug soon after this.

Salmon Fisheries

The Rivers Torridge, Taw, Ex, Teigh, and Tamar all had summer salmon fisheries worked by men on a part time basis. Heavy clinker boats were rowed or sailed over long distances to carry the cotton nets. Once the light monofilament nets came in they didn't need the heavy wooden boats, but several are still in use.

The Tamar licence originally allowed salmon to be taken on the Tamar, Tavy and Lynher, but this area has gradually been cut back to the Tamar, below Cotehele. Because of declining fish stocks the Cornwall River Board sort in 1962 to reduce the number of licences issued, but in 1974 the South West Water cut the number back to just fifteen licences, There has been controversy between conservationists and traditional fishermen to keep the fishery going.

Aboard the smack *Shamrock* with *Velsia* astern in the 1978 Dartmouth Old Gaffer's Race.

Because the seine nets are worked by hand the men need a hard standing foreshore. There are thirteen of these stations on the Cornish side of the river and nine on the Devon shore. Each station has its own name and many have not been worked for years. The salmon are mostly netted on low water neaps when the tide is not too strong, but by 2000 the catches were very low.

Yachts anchored off the north end of Torre Abbey Sands, Tor Bay in 1888 waiting for the owners to come aboard. In the Victorian period the great yachts with their paid crews sailed around the coast attending the grand regattas. The regattas at Torquay were held in August.

Brixham Trawlers

In 1759 a group at Brixham bought the harbour from the Lord of the Manor. The successors to this group, known as the 'Quay Lords and Ladies', continued to run the harbour until about 1925. Originally Brixham was little more than a cove at the side of Tor Bay, but the Eastern Quay was built in 1795 and this is now part of the inner harbour. Brixham's fleet of trawlers grew to such numbers that there was not room for them all in the harbour. In bad weather many smacks had to anchor off the harbour and some were driven ashore and wrecked. During one north east gale in 1866 sixty craft were lost in the harbour and over hundred lives. Many ships were driven right up into the streets and women lit a bonfire, after the lighthouse had been washed away, to try and guide vessels making for the harbour.

Work to extend the outer breakwater did not start in earnest until about 1892. To pay for the cost of this, a levy of three pence was put on every pound's worth of fish sold at Brixham. The work was slow and the breakwater was not completed until 1912.

The fishermen of Brixham developed trawling which, since it involved dragging a net along the seabed, required a powerful craft. Although Cornish luggers used the harbour for landing fish, the Brixham men always used gaff-rigged trawlers and these were some of the most seaworthy craft used in western Europe, as they had to survive at sea in all weathers. Because they worked in the long Altantic swell of the English Channel and Bristol Channel, the Brixham trawlers had their main mast stepped well aft. In correct nautical terminology the later Brixham trawlers were gaff ketches, but in 'The Bay' they were called 'dandys.' The smaller 70 footers were known as 'mules' or 'Mumble bees' while those around 78ft long were first class smacks.

As Brixham was a long way from the coalmines, steam trawlers were too expensive to operate. Most of the Brixham smacks were in 'single ship ownership' and there was simply not the capital in the town to buy steam trawlers.

The great era of smack building was around 1900 and in 1912 R. Jackson built his last smack, the 80ft *Terminist*, at his yard near the Brixham Breakwater. Jackson also built the *Maid Honour* which, during World War II, was sailed to the West Coast of Africa by special forces that captured three Italian ships.

There was a revival of smack building after World War I to replace wartime losses. Jackson built the *Torbay Lass* in 1923. The *Torbay Lass* received a good salvage reward when she towed the Bideford three-masted schooner *Welcome* into Mount's Bay in fourteen hours from seven miles south-west of the Wolf Rock.

The last Brixham smack built by J.W. & A. Upham was the 78ft *Vigilance* in 1926. She was built at a cost £1000 for the Foster brothers and they followed the traditional pattern of fishing. Trawling from Brixham in the winter, moving to Mount's Bay in March and then moving around to the Bristol Channel and landing their fish at Tenby. The last smack built at Brixham was *Ruby Eileen* in 1927.

In the inter-war Depression Brixham's trawlers only just kept going and the number of boats fishing fell steadily and did not revive until power craft were introduced after World War II. By 1935 there were only fifteen first class smacks owned at Brixham and very few were actually fishing. The *Girl Inez*, lost by fire off the Irish coast, is believed to have been the last one fishing under sail.

Several almost new smacks were sold as yachts, often for less than their cost of building. About forty Brixham trawlers were sold to become yachts and in 2003 there were about eighteen Brixham trawlers still afloat. Most were far from their home port, such as the *Deodar*, built by Jackson in 1911, which was sold to Lowestoft and then on to Norwegian owners and is now based in Stockholm.

In the days of a sailing fishing fleet at Brixham most smacks returned home in August to fit out for the winter, and some took part in the Brixham Trawler Race. In 1919 Captain Jones' *Sunny Isle* was the first winner of the King George V Perpetual Challenge Trophy and a letter was sent to King George saying the gift was a link between the Port of Brixham and the Throne. This race was reported in the national papers and Brixham and her trawlers became well known, far beyond Tor Bay. The 78ft *Valerian* won most of these races in the 1920s. During World War II the *Valerian* was one of the trawlers that was moored with a barrage balloon above her to prevent enemy aircraft bombing big cities.

In tough financial times it was difficult to keep the race going, but in 1933 seven trawlers raced in the regatta. The race was sailed in strong winds and the *Vigilance* won, just ahead of the *Torbay Lass*. The next day seven brown-sailed smacks raced for the Albert Wallace Memorial Cup, which *Forsetti* won.

A Brixham trawler in Tor Bay in about 1934.

In 1937 the Fosters could no longer make fishing under sail pay and the *Vigilance* was sold by auction to Percy Upham. She was laid up until 1949 when she became a yacht. She had a short career as a yacht because her owner was drowned. On the day of his cremation a mysterious fire almost destroyed the smack. It was believed that the man's widow had set fire to her to prevent her son from using the *Vigilance*. Perhaps the most amazing part of the smack's history is that Ken Harris devoted some forty-two years to restoring her. In 1997 the Vigilance of Brixham Preservation Company purchased the *Vigilance* and brought her back to Brixham.

After a period of around sixty years, Brixham trawlers began to return home. In 1999 trawler skipper Bill Wakeham brought the *Pilgrim* back to Brixham and converted her back to sail. The *Pilgrim* had been built by Upham's at Brixham in 1895 and when her fishing career was over she had been sold to Danish owners and converted to a power craft.

There were enough trawlers in sailing order to keep the races going until just before World War II. In 1953 the races were revived for trawlers converted to yachts over a 17 mile course around Tor Bay. Only three took part, the *Provident* won the first day's racing while the *Rulewater*, built at Brixham in 1917, won the second day, but the remaining trawlers were scattered over such a wide area that it was impossible to get enough there to race. It was not until 1997 that racing for the King George V Trophy was revived and sailed in Tor Bay. The 2002 race in Brixham Heritage Week was won by *Vigilance* (1926) and other former trawlers which entered were the *Leader* (1892) *Pilgrim* (1895) *Keewaydin* (1913) *Kenya Jacaranda ex-Torbay Lass* (1923) *Provident* (1924)). The *Our Daddy* won the new class for luggers.

The Brixham trawler *Vigilance* in the 1978 Dartmouth Old Gaffers Race.

The Brixham trawler *Pilgrim* on Alan Toms' slips at Polruan in 2001.

Also from Creekside Publishing by Robert Simper.

English Estuaries Series

DEBEN RIVER
RIVER ORWELL AND RIVER STOUR
RIVERS ALDE, ORE AND BLYTH
NORFOLK RIVERS AND HARBOURS
ESSEX RIVERS AND CREEKS
THAMES TIDEWAY
RIVER MEDWAY AND THE SWALE
RIVERS TO THE FENS

The Sea and the Land books

IN SEARCH OF SAIL
FAMILY FIELDS
VOYAGE AROUND EAST ANGLIA
WOODBRIDGE & BEYOND

The Coast in the Past Series

FORGOTTEN COAST
SUNRISE COAST